Dancing on Mars

Lucinda Shirley

ALL THINGS THAT MATTER PRESS

Dancing on Mars

ISBN: 978-0-9850066-1-7

Library of Congress Control Number: 2012933998

Cover art by Lucinda Shirley
Author photo by Laura Lee

Cover design by All Things That Matter Press

Published in 2012 by All Things That Matter Press

For my mother
with great love

and in memory
of my father
whom I sorely miss.

Acknowledgments

Abiding gratitude

to Deb and Phil Harris at All Things That Matter Press - For believing this book should be published even though, like its author, *Dancing on Mars* resists labels and doesn't conform to a specific literary niche.

to Coleman Barks for permission to quote Rumi (*The Essential Rumi* translated by Coleman Barks, copyright 1995, Coleman Barks, HarperSanFrancisco). You can visit the esteemed poet and translator of Rumi at colemanbarks.com.

to "Neal" - Your unconditional love and support are deeply treasured in this and all things, precious son.

to "Jack" for helping me heal my life and find the courage to live it authentically. Rest in peace, my friend.

to Pat Mikelson who knows me well and honors our longtime friendship by telling me the truth, always. *Dancing on Mars* is a better book because of your wise counsel and support. Special thanks, dear friend.

to Vicki Dodds, Anita Floyd and Paula Hines—good friends and lovers of books—for your time, patience, and invaluable insights throughout this process.

to the amazing anonymous humans who were willing to be interviewed and to those who responded to my questions about being married or single, and to the "voices from longtime marriages." You honored me with your generosity and your candor, and I'm grateful for your friendship. Readers will benefit immensely from your sharing.

to those who visited the blogs: Every visit, every comment, every e-mail mean so much—still.

to my dear friend Jodie McCord and "faerie goddaughter" Laura Lee - I don't know what I would have done without your help and support. To Patricia Johnson, Fran Massa George, Adrienne Molloy, Audrey Baxter, Belleruth Naparstek, Roz Adams, Cora Plass, Sara Davidson, Marjorie Wentworth, and Cassie Premo Steele who were "there for me" in many and various ways, I thank you!

to the friends and neighbors who have made this a sweeter experience by offering to host book signings, by inviting me to your book clubs and—most of all—saying you'll buy the book and spread the word about it. I am humbled by, and immensely grateful for, your generous support.

Part I

If Wishes Were Horses

One good wish changes nothing; one good decision changes everything." ~ Anonymous

The Reluctant Thespian

When were the auditions?
I didn't try out for the part.
This play—no, I must say
I do much better with farce.

This mask chokes off my air—
Who wrote the script? How long ago?
I understand that nothing's fair,
But I don't want to do this show.

When were the auditions?
I'm really not right for the part—
The audience is seated?
Yes, I'm standing on my mark.

Everybody except the beach party chaperone had left for the Pavilion by the time my mother and her friend Isabelle finished primping. The two stragglers walked toward the main road knowing their hair and starched cotton didn't stand a chance in the South Carolina humidity.

When Isabelle wished for a car, my mother said, "If wishes were horses, beggars would ride." That's when Isabelle thought of hitchhiking. It was in love's best interest that social standards were relaxed during wartime.

As it turned out, Fate sent these beggars a convertible with two fellows in it, students at the University, happy to give them a lift. They were headed to the Pavilion, too. My father was the handsome one in the passenger seat, a ringer for young Brando.

Later that night "Brando" boasted to his friend, "I'm gonna marry that little girl." And he did, two days after finishing Midshipman School at Northwestern. They had a sweet wedding on a freezing night just after Christmas; the church was so cold Mama's teeth chattered through the whole ceremony. The newlyweds had only a few days together before my father reported for Navy duty, but three days were all they needed to plant the seed that eventually would be me.

My father was stationed in California while my mother lived pregnantly at her mother's house. After a couple of months, Mama took a train from South Carolina to the West Coast to visit her new husband. I think it was courageous for a nineteen-year-old with morning sickness to make that long, rattly train trip. Her courage was fueled by the power of young love.

When Mama got to California, she and Papa shared a single bed in the basement bedroom of a wealthy San Diego widow. Mama told me about standing with Papa at a bus stop, waiting for a ride to La Jolla. A number of buses stopped, but not one to La Jolla. When their bus didn't come and didn't come, they asked someone whether the bus would be stopping at that corner. They learned that a La Jolla bus had come and gone several times while they waited. They had been looking for a different spelling, something involving an "h" and maybe a "y." Babes in the woods, those two.

My mother advertised for a ride back to South Carolina and got one with three officers' wives. It must have been a long trip, pregnant and in the company of older women she didn't know, and in a 1943 sedan.

***

To this day Mama still says, "I declare you were grown when you were born. You never were a chile."

I don't believe my young parents were ready for a "chile" when I came along in that first year of the marriage. Not that I wasn't welcome once I got here. I was born in South Carolina, nine months and two days after the nuptials. My father was still on the West Coast, and I didn't meet him until I was six months old. Everyone said I looked exactly like him, not that there was a question of paternity. You'd know that if you knew my mother. Mama recalls taking me to the train station to greet Papa the day he came back from California. She had me all dressed up in a little pink coat and bonnet. By the time Papa arrived, there I was with a red, tear-streaked face, screaming bloody murder. So much for first impressions.

There was a reason Papa came back to South Carolina before the war ended. As a Navy ensign, he had orders to ship out when an ear infection intervened. Those orders were canceled when his eardrum burst. The ship left without him and didn't make it back. There were no survivors.

***

My mother had two sisters; she was in the middle. When she was nine, her father, a medical doctor, was diagnosed as Paranoid Schizophrenic. After years of prying for answers to help me understand her earlier life, and therefore my mother as a woman, she told me something significant. At about age ten, she had witnessed her hysterical father being taken away in a straight jacket to a veteran's hospital in Georgia where he would remain until his death. It was clear Mama didn't want me making a fuss over the unexpected gift of truth she had just given me, so I didn't express the sadness I was feeling. Or the shock. The fact that my grandfather suffered mental illness had been a secret, or maybe more of a mystery. When I was growing up, no one would talk about what happened to him, and I learned not to ask. I overheard fragments of whispered conversations, just enough to feel confused and suspect that the adults in my life—the people I needed to trust—were lying. I have some memory of being told my grandfather had contracted TB. At one point it was implied that he was no longer living, which of course he was. Sadly, there was an aura of shame around the subject of mental illness then, far more than today. Thankfully, our culture has become more educated on the subject.

When Mama told me about her father, we were just finishing lunch at our favorite restaurant in Columbia. I took a sip of sweet tea and a deep breath. Mama had been her father's pet, and he had confused her with one of her sisters when she visited him in the hospital. My heart ached for the little girl who was my mother. I finally understood why seeing someone she loves express strong emotions would trigger fear and feelings of helplessness. It explained a lot. Including why I always have felt protective, have nurtured her as if she were my child instead of the other way around.

Mama grew up under the influence of a stoic, Victorian mother and her mother's parents and siblings. They all lived on the same street someone nicknamed Squirrel Ridge. Combine the loss of her father with the Victorian element and her strict religious training, and it's easy to see she didn't stand much chance of reaching adulthood unscathed.

I have no doubt that, as a child and even as an adult, I taught my grandmama Mammy to accept affection. I'm physically demonstrative with people I love; I like hugs. Mammy never did surrender to a hug completely, but she gave up on avoiding them. I know she enjoyed the attention I gave her. She just wasn't big on being touched, nor was Mama.

It's highly doubtful Mama was hugged much as she was growing up. I'm told I was held and cuddled by my parents when I was an infant and young child. But by the time I reached school age, Mama's body would stiffen when I hugged her. With time, she learned to appreciate an embrace; now she even relaxes into them a little. I remember the first time she hugged me long enough for *me* to think about letting go. That was major.

***

My father was the youngest of eight children and lived, until his father's death, on their small farm in south Georgia. During the Great Depression the family couldn't hold on to the farm, and Papa's father passed away around that same time. Papa was sent to live with his oldest sister and her husband in South Carolina. I wanted to know about his childhood, always probing for pieces of his life. It was like trying to excise an embedded splinter to get him to share anything much about his past. But he finally told me a little about that time in his boyhood.

He said my aunt and uncle were good to him. I knew their son, more than ten years younger than my father, and it was obvious he looked up to Papa with affectionate admiration. Papa had a paper route and was working three jobs by the time he got to high school. And, he became the first student body president at that brand-new school.

Just as I was beginning to get a sense of his life at that time, Papa said something funny to derail more significant sharing. I inherited his ability to invoke humor to avoid intimacy.

Even though his sister and her husband were "good" to him, it had to be tough for a boy to be uprooted from his family, from his home. But he told me nothing about his feelings. Any time I would ask him, or Mama, how they *felt* about this or that, they'd look confused. You'd think I had asked how they like grilled chipmunk or something. They truly didn't understand my question.

***

When I think about Mama and Papa and their histories, I wonder how they turned out as well as they did. Mama could easily be a complete basket case, and Papa might have become a bitter, miserly soul instead of the exact opposite. Fairly healthy people, considering. Maybe they made life manageable by keeping their emotions walled off and locked up tight.

In talking about parenting recently, my mother said she had wanted most of all for her children to love her. That's why she did everything possible to please us, to make our lives "easy." She was usually patient, except when we'd get hurt. Then sometimes she'd get angry and scold us, especially if we cried. Because of what she had told me about her father, I understand that now.

Mama was more than willing to bail us out of any challenging or unpleasant experiences. With my first brush with performance anxiety, before a piano recital, Mama told my music teacher I was sick and unable to perform. I never knew, until well into adulthood, that I could be scared about doing something and still accomplish the thing I was afraid of doing.

When any excitement was expected on "Days of Our Lives," Mama would let me stay home or get out of school early to watch the soap opera. The good stuff usually happened on Fridays. She had no clue that her indulgences weren't in our best interest. I don't fault her intentions, but she could have used some help with judgment on occasion. I wish she could have known then that her children would love her no matter what, even if she had imposed some rules and said "no" sometimes.

***

Without a doubt, my mother is the most generous person I know. She was tied for first place in the generosity category before my father passed away. Now she's the sole title holder.

Generally speaking, Mama's an easy-going, passive person. Aggression kicks in only in rare cases of frustration or anger. I realized a few years ago that I've said some outrageous, sometimes borderline cruel, things to provoke her into showing emotion—anger, tears, anything. I've never seen my mother cry. Never. She says she cries at "sweet things," and I have seen her eyes puddle up during sentimental movies. Not long ago she said she does cry sometimes, but only in private. I was relieved when she told me that.

She usually keeps her regularly-scheduled appointments at the beauty parlor, but she won't keep a calendar. So she sometimes misses things that are less significant to her, doctor appointments and such. She refuses to have an alarm clock in her room. Instead, she designates somebody to wake her if she needs to get up at a certain time. If she goes back to sleep after the wake-up call, it's not her fault. Someone should have made sure she was up.

Talking with my mother on the phone today, the subject of her wake-up calls arose, and I learned something: Mama won't have a clock in her room because it makes her think about her life ticking away too fast. There's "just something inside her" that resists it, and she doesn't know why she feels that way. I was happy to trade years of judgmental assumption for some understanding. It felt good to know the clock thing has been about her feelings all along, rather than refusal to take personal responsibility.

Mama's a championship listener, interested in whatever her children tell her, no matter how trivial or outrageous. She's still a big reader, and I'm grateful that my own love of reading is strong because of her influence. She encouraged me to read when I was very young, and later I nearly wore out the sidewalks between our house and the Library.

I struggled for years to figure out who I am, wanting to uncover "the real me." That caused some upheaval in our symbiotic relationship, but Mama still gave me her support. Even though the concepts of introspection and serious self-examination terrified her, she encouraged me throughout my own therapeutic process.

Except for her long-ago-and-nearly-forgotten fears for my endangered soul, Mama has been my greatest cheerleader. Even as I discarded mask after mask, and she must have had trouble recognizing me, she never kicked me out of her heart. I know I hurt her during those years. I still do on occasion. And she still can hurt me. Ours is a rare and complicated bond; at times it has felt like bondage. But the important thing is that our bond is sealed with unconditional love. There's nothing stronger than that.

***

Like most marriages, my parents' relationship experienced some rocky times. Mama still tells anyone who mentions divorce that she wishes she'd been able to leave Papa on a few occasions. The reason she didn't, she says, was her lack of job skills; maybe that's why she wanted to be sure I learned to type. I have no doubt that the good far outweighed the bad in their sixty-plus years together.

By the time I was eleven or twelve, one parent sometimes would take me aside to air grievances about the other. A couple of times, when she was really vexed, Mama told me not to let Papa in the house when he got home that night. He'd been coming home from the Legislature really late, and she was determined to act out a full range of passive aggression. He knocked on my window, waking me to unlock the door when he realized she had locked him out. You see, we didn't lock our doors back then. Nobody did.

Being involved in their marriage was complicated. It was torturous having my loyalty divided that way. She and Papa both treated me like a peer most of the time, so it was confusing, at best, when they'd suddenly shift gears and treat me as whatever age I was. As far as the family went, consistency was something I couldn't count on. My inner world was chaotic, and I did everything in my power to see that the family's external reality didn't match the chaos that lived in me. My anxious need for control would see to it.

***

It was wonderful to see my parents fall in love all over again in their sixties. Not that they ever fell out of love. After about four decades together, they grew into the fullness of love, plus something that seemed brand new. You could see it when they looked at each other, hear it when they teased back and forth.

In his late sixties, my father—who had put most of his energy into working hard and playing harder— began wanting my mother to be with him as much as possible. He even wanted her in the room while watching sports on his three or four TV sets. She seemed pleased about that. Our den looked like a Best Buy or the electronics department at Wal-Mart, and Papa always placed bets on football games just to "make 'em more interesting to watch." I would be mortified when he'd say out loud in public, "Come on, let's go. I need to call my bookie."

My parents went through some years of having their evening

cocktails during *Wheel of Fortune* and *Jeopardy*. Papa still was able to play golf then, but he'd come home a lot earlier than he used to. Probably he passed up the gin rummy afterwards. Mama continues to have my admiration for being willing and able to read with sounds of all sorts blasting from his TV's. Remember, Papa was deaf in one ear, so there was considerable amplification.

My father had the world's greatest sense of humor and a disarming manner that endeared him to just about everybody. I'm ever grateful to have his sense of humor and the ability to find something funny in the darkest of circumstances.

He was a Yellow Dog Democrat because he "cared about people." His compassion was reflected in the way he practiced law and in his Legislative service. I think he balanced self-confidence and humility pretty well. He never was pretentious, and he had a contagious zest for life. He joked around with us a lot; I don't think Papa took anything about us too seriously when we were growing up. Mama was in charge of worrying.

Mama has a wry, subtle sense of humor. It's still evident in her life today. Humor always has been welcome at our house. But you knew better than to let your anger show, and tears would frustrate both Mama and Papa in a big way. Neither parent wanted to take on the role of bad cop either, although they were forced to assume it on rare occasions.

I have some second-hand memories, stories people have told me about when I was a child. But much of my own memory is blocked, as if someone pulled a blackout shade over parts of it. In reflecting on my parents, I can see that they did the very best they could have done. Who can expect more than that?

***

Sidebar: Later in life Papa became a dedicated family man. By then he fully appreciated what a gem Mama was, and he began acting as if his whole family was of primary importance, too. Even though we were in various stages of middle age by then. It took him a while, but he finally fulfilled the *Father Knows Best* fantasies we had growing up. There's some truth to the saying "It's never too late to have a happy childhood."

He and Mama would host monthly dinners at an oriental restaurant in Columbia. He'd send full-page memos typed by his secretary, with details spelled out as carefully as in a legal document. We would gather at my house or one of my brothers' for drinks before going to dinner. My sister lives out of state and was able to join us only on rare occasions.

Papa made some of our childhood wishes come true by organizing two weekend trips to a State Park where we each had our own room with a view, enjoyed dinner at a multi-star restaurant in the nearest town, then saw a play at a community theater just down the street. He even hit tennis balls with us the next morning. Papa made all the plans with great care, in the interest of giving us maximum pleasure. Pleasure was high on his priority list, and he wanted us to have plenty of it. Those TV families would have envied us then.

***

Brother was born a little more than two years after I came along, then my sister came four years after Brother. Apparently I was sometimes proprietary, acting as the "other mother" in the household. My siblings would be unanimous in telling you I was bossy and controlling. Truth be told, I was completely overwhelmed by them, feeling a burden of responsibility far beyond the ability or power of my years. My bossiness was something like whistling in the graveyard on a dark night.

Even as a young child, I somehow felt I should know the right thing to say and do in every circumstance. So I would gauge other people's moods and behave accordingly. I learned to be a diplomat, and I knew how to entertain the grownups. I could make them laugh from the time I was very young. I'm told that relatives, friends, and neighbors would stop by Mammy's house to hear me talk. My claim to family fame is that I was talking, even saying a few sentences, before I could sit up on my own.

I grew up in the small town where generations of Mama's family had lived. We stayed with Mammy until I was about five so Papa could finish his Navy obligations and then study law at the University of South Carolina. After the years at Mammy's, we moved into a two-bedroom prefabricated house on the street behind hers; Papa had been able to buy it through the GI bill. A well-worn path connected our back yard to Mammy's. There were two, then three of us, in the second bedroom of the little house. The bathroom was about the size of a closet.

Papa's mother, Big Mama, came to visit when we lived there, and I think she came a couple of times after we moved to Carlisle Avenue. As you might imagine, she was a large woman, down-to-earth and affectionate. She kept an enamel, bowl-shaped potty under the bed, a "slop jar" she called it. I guess that was in case the bathroom was occupied when she had an urgent need. And maybe she was not yet accustomed to indoor plumbing, since they had used an outhouse on the farm for years. I think I would remember if she had used her slop jar, since she stayed in the room with Brother and me. It would have made an impression to see that, accustomed as I was to an extremely modest mother.

Big Mama drank something called Postum, brought it with her on the bus from Jacksonville. That's about all I remember, except that she called my father "Bubba." We went to Jacksonville a couple of times to see Big Mama and visited Papa's two older brothers there. We'd be packed in Papa's car, all six of us, seven when Emma came along. Both of his brothers were almost as sweet as Papa; they had worked hard and become wealthy. I'm pretty sure they were Republicans. I don't know when Big Mama died or what caused her death. I don't remember any emotions around her leaving this world, probably because she wasn't a primary presence in my world.

One of the best things about that time and place was being allowed to roam freely around the neighborhood and eventually around town. We loved going barefoot as soon as the weather was warm enough "for butter to melt on the table."

Southern Childhood Revisited

Vital signs were stronger then
when bare feet pounded prayers
into pavement,
when Crepe Myrtle and Queen Anne's Lace
decorated the long summers.
Our night lanterns were fireflies
in mason-jar cells.
We didn't think of them
as prisoners,
did not think of ourselves
as free.

Cloud pictures—horses changing into old men
in a magic shift of wind, Abraham Lincoln once,
stovepipe hat and all.

Covering a talcumed neck with kisses
for a stick of Juicy Fruit,
sitting out eternities on church pews
stifling yawns and giggles.
A dime for the Saturday picture show
& money under the table
from Aunt Helen for popcorn.

Soon as butter would melt on the table
bare feet found their way into clover,
running like the wind from a bull
in the pasture
Red Rover, Red Rover ...

Listening to tales in chairs
that rocked beneath the stars,
listening to crickets when the talk
got around to people dying.
The crickets were real.

Tarzan hiding in backyard trees,
Jane licking warm chocolate
from a wooden spoon,
Loves-me-loves-me-not with rose petals,
always ending with "loves me."
Red Rover, Red Rover...

Red sky at night mean the world gonna end
by mawnin'....
Flour-covered fingers erasing tears,
a gumdrop to stop the flow.

Where did it go, that kind of childhood?
Was it mine or have I somehow

confused it with my mother's?

Red Rover, Red Rover
Let my son come over.

***

Emma was a major part of the up-side of life then, unless we caused her displeasure. We knew to steer clear of her then. At age twelve Emma began coming to our house when her day at "the school for colored children" ended. She would look after us and help Mama some. Later, Emma would end up running the household, taking over much of my "other mother" role. She would sometimes shame Papa into making decisions about home repairs he wasn't enthusiastic about. He seemed to think you just built a house and that was it, nothing further to do. He never assigned much importance to maintenance, but Emma and Mama would team up and get things done.

When Emma was beyond childhood, she and Papa would bet on the World Series. Every year he'd take the American League, she, the National. They ribbed each other a lot. Without exception, everybody who came to our house for dinner bragged on Emma's cooking and took second helpings. Her biscuits were so light, I'm pretty sure they could float. Emma was my go-to friend and confidante all of her life, one of the trinity of women I lived to please. I learned a lot about self-sufficiency from her. She had no problem shaming me into it, but I wouldn't grow up helpless if she had anything to do with it. Few days go by that I don't say *Thank you, Emma,* even after all these years since her passing.

Growing up, I was most comfortable when I was in a controlling mode. It was, of course, only an illusion of having control over the life going on around me. There sometimes was confusion and tension in my relationships with the adults in my life. There was Mammy's puzzling rigidity, coupled with words of affection, and the risk that came with saying or doing something in an effort to make her smile or laugh. I turned myself inside out to gather "real" evidence that she loved me, that I was special to her. I felt her love far more often than not.

Then there were Mama's generous indulgences paired with criticism, declarations of love sometimes followed by critical words in the same sentence; "backhanded compliments" we call that in the South. Papa's affectionate teasing and helping with my math homework alternated with his self-involvement and indifference to the family at times. That's when I felt invisible to him; yet at other times he made me feel special. He said many times, "You know you're the apple of my eye." I see that I'm describing life in extremes, and that's what I experienced.

Emma's moody on-again, off-again warmth and approval would be coupled, at times, with scorn. Usually I felt Emma's love, but there was resentment, too. Not necessarily resentment towards me or us. I believe a lot of that was about the social, racial dynamic we co-existed with. And why wouldn't she resent it? None of it made sense, and I found it disturbing in many ways. I felt embarrassment and shame that our races were separate, even though we didn't feel "separate" from Emma and her family. Yet it was the only way of life I had known.

My confusion around the adults' behavior made the closest relationships in my world seem unreliable in one way or another.

Years later I was at Emma's bedside with my mother and Emma's daughters when she left this world. Before her girls arrived at the hospital, I stood beside her as she slept. Or maybe she was officially in a coma. I felt she had some awareness. I had heard one shouldn't say things to the dying that might keep the spirit from setting itself free. I also understood that we sometimes need to give people permission to go. With my hand over hers I began to sing in a near-whisper, "Oooh Oooh child, things are gonna get easier, oooh child things will get brighter ...." I wasn't exactly channeling Nina Simone, but my voice was better than it ever had been. Being with Emma during her transition to spirit was an honor. It was the most profoundly intimate experience of my life so far, deeply humbling. I'll always be grateful that her daughters wanted us to share that intimacy with them, that they were willing to share Emma with us until the very end. I loved Emma dearly, and I continue to miss her. Her "girls" and I stay in touch.

***

After a short time in our little house, my parents added a pine-paneled den. I liked that it was paneled. I imagined movie stars had rooms like that. And the best thing about it was the fireplace.

Smoke & Mirrors

Winter chimney tops
become the smoke & mirrors
of memory,
freezing nights longer then
when we warmed our boney selves
at Mama's fire
built with coal and useless papers
twisted into spirals.

We were long in bed
when she took up the ashes,
leaning into herself,
listening
for my father's old Pontiac.

We were long in bed
but one of us
was not sleeping.
One small girl,
impotent guardian
of the mother's heart,
lay still as stone
breathing less than her
portion of common air
in the little room.

Morning fireplace
was black again
empty
as if it never gave birth
to warmth at all
or made goodness
with its light.

Icy feet

would forget
until a smudge of ash
on Mama's brow
reminded us,
gave rise to a longing
for its sacred return.

***

The downside to being me in that time and place was the total lack of privacy and all the household noise. There was no stillness, ever. I remember having little to call my own for very long. Toys would get broken; pages in favorite books would disappear or be mutilated. I couldn't seem to have anything nice. Whatever I had, someone would either take it or break it. Par for the sibling course, I suppose.

My parents built a house a few blocks from my grandmother's when I was eleven. Mama drew the plans herself while Papa was busy practicing law and serving in the Legislature. Once we moved into the larger house the family grew larger, too. Before I turned twelve, we had a baby brother. 'D' would remain the youngest of the four children.

In the new house on Carlisle Avenue, I had a room of my own. I treasured having a door that was mine and the power to close it. Of course sometimes there were trespassers. Maybe that's why I've always needed and appreciated space of my very own.

Right after baby D was born, I stayed home from school a few days to change diapers and serve Mama Campbell's tomato soup with saltine crackers for lunch. For some reason Emma wasn't there, and I was in charge. Every time I changed D's tiny diaper, I was horrified that the remaining stump of drying umbilical cord would break off. It didn't. The visiting nurse was there to deal with "it" when it happened.

***

Even in grainy black and white home movies it's easy to see how proprietary and protective I was with Brother. In one movie he's toddling around Mammy's front yard, and I'm there to catch him when he loses his balance. In another, I'm more or less dragging Brother along, attempting to pick him up when he fell. He could've gotten up on his own, but mostly he tolerated my ministrations. If he cried, I would soothe and distract him. He was a handsome little fellow. An adult cousin began calling him "Red Truck," because that was his favorite toy; he could say "red truck" before he was talking much. Thankfully the nickname didn't stick for long.

Brother was a clever kid. One time he made sure Mammy heard him praying for a horse. One time was all it took. He didn't have to worry about God coming through as long as Mammy was around. Very soon an old white horse named "Silver" became Brother's pet. Our pet. You might have guessed by now that Brother was Mammy's pet.

Brother's sense of humor was and is sharp, and he's a great mimic, like Mammy. In high school, he and some friends started a band, and Brother was one of the singers. They got to be pretty good, even played some gigs in Columbia. He could have passed for one of the Temptations if you had a couple of beers and closed your eyes: "I've got sunshine on a cloudy day ...." Guess where they rehearsed their wide-open rock and roll? Mammy's house.

I always have felt a strong connection to Brother, loved him even when it didn't show. That was mostly when I was worried about him. He and I would laugh at the same things and could say most anything to each other when I wasn't obsessing about his well-being. I'd act like a bitch when I felt impotent.

"Happy Tooth," my sister who's six years younger, actually became a dentist. She was cute as could be, but she wouldn't stay still long enough to be doted on. She could wiggle out of your lap before you could blink twice. We kept a collective eye out so we wouldn't find her on top of the refrigerator or "washing dishes," starting with the carving knife *again*. We had no idea how she monkeyed her way onto or into seemingly impossible places.

When I was not quite twelve and our parents were away for a few days, Mammy was staying nights at our house. It was summer, and there were some hours in the day when there was no adult around. I guess I was considered the adult supervision then. Sister came home from wherever she had been playing, just after getting a hard blow to her head. She began throwing up, and I was the only one at home.

Emma had gone to her own home after dinner to take care of Miss Sissy, her disabled mother. I'm guessing they didn't have a phone back then, or no doubt I'd have called her. Mammy was playing bridge somewhere. It was mid-afternoon. I called our doctor, a distant cousin and neighbor. Doc made a house call, concluding that Happy Tooth had suffered a concussion. Under no circumstances was I to allow her to fall asleep because she "might not wake up." I knew that meant she would die, and it was up to me to make sure she didn't. A big yellow ceramic bowl was at the bedside to accommodate her occasional heaving, and I sat on the edge of the bed talking to her. I was attempting a delicate balance of soothing her, but not so much that her eyes would close for more than a second. I think I put cool compresses on her forehead, but I'm not sure. I am sure I did whatever Doc had told me to do. She kept trying to sleep. I was determined not to let my sister sleep or sense the terror I was feeling. When Mammy came that evening, I was relieved. We took turns playing nurse until whatever hour Doc had said it would be safe to call a halt to our vigil.

In first grade my sister told her teacher that boys had been using the girls' restroom. She didn't know the boys who were using it. Teachers and principal took turns monitoring the door.

After a couple of days, the teacher questioned Sister in greater detail, finally asking exactly how she knew that boys had been using the girls' restroom since she hadn't actually seen the boys. It was obvious, Sister told her: The toilet seats had been turned up.

Sister was a sucker for stray animals and brought home many a cat and dog. Just hours before my wedding rehearsal she climbed a tree to rescue a cat, and the Fire Department had to get them both down. She was about thirteen at the time.

In family of origin therapy, Baby D, as he grew into boyhood, would fit the role of "mascot." Something like a court jester. He was fun and funny, mostly wanting to be loved by everybody. I, for one, loved him dearly. Sometimes it seemed as if he were my own child. He was adorable, always clowning around, singing, entertaining us with jokes and hamming it up in general. He craved attention. He would stay up sometimes and watch "The Late Show" with Mama while she waited for Papa to come home from Columbia.

D wasn't the monkey Sister was, but he got into his share of mischief. One day he decided to give Clyde, his pet snake, a change of scenery. Clyde escaped from D's room and disappeared somewhere in the house. The reptilian terrorist kept us on high alert for weeks. We never did find him. My guess is he either made it to the outdoors or there's a disintegrating snakeskin behind the breakfront in the dining room.

D was passionate about his CB radio when he was eleven or twelve. His radio name was "Golden Eagle." I remember a picture of D in a football uniform, handsome and trying to look mean; next day there was a picture taken with his new leg cast. That might have been the end of his athletic pursuits.

Mama usually took individual requests for supper, and I thought it was a mistake for her to cater to "the children" that way. When we were growing up, "dinner" meant the main meal in the middle of the day, and Emma always cooked a big one. Sometimes leftovers were part of the evening's short-order options. Brother wouldn't eat anything green; D pretty much survived on Vienna sausages and applesauce. I'm not sure Happy Tooth ever paused long enough to eat. There was a period of having the evening meal together, outdoors at our new picnic table, but we usually would have our supper whenever we wanted and eat it anywhere. It was a lot of extra work for Mama and didn't do much toward preparing them for the real world. I usually ate supper in my room while I was doing homework or reading. Once we moved to the new house, I often called Mammy to say goodnight; I'm remembering that her phone number was 251!

***

In high school I got the responsible jobs, like editor of the newspaper and business manager of this or that. All I wanted, just once, was to do the more frivolous things, like ride on the homecoming float and wave to the crowd from a convertible in the Christmas parade or, best of all, be a cheerleader. It just wasn't in the cards. I was heckled at cheerleader tryouts by some older boys who mocked my husky voice when it was my turn to perform. Thankfully, I don't remember how few votes I got. That audition was my last voluntary public humiliation.

I dated one boy at a time, a "steady." I wasn't sexually active unless you'd count soulful kisses with the steady boyfriend. With the one I was really crazy about, "in love" with, there was some awkward groping—on his part, not mine. And I felt terribly guilty about that. Mama had warned me more than once that it would "kill" her and "kill Mammy" if anything ever "happened" with a boy before I was married. The boys only wanted one thing, she said; if you gave it to them, they'd "drop" you. Kick you to the curb like so much trash, which you probably were. I took that to heart, the place where residual fear and guilt are stored, all mixed up in a jumble with the love.

Sidebar: My parents never were strict. Mama just "trusted" me to do the right thing. They didn't set a curfew or make other rules to guide me. She believed trusting me was a good thing. A compliment, I suppose. But I didn't have the skills or maturity to navigate all the situations I would face. Having the structure of rules, knowing what the limits were, would have helped. I made my own rules and was harder on myself than they'd ever have been. I still am sometimes.

I polled friends to find out how late they were allowed to be out on date nights and borrowed a reasonable curfew. No one knew I set my own, starting at thirteen. Yes, I was dating then. In fact, I got my driver's license at fourteen and drove Mammy to Charleston the next day. We stayed with my aunt, and I went to a dance at The Citadel with a blind date, the roommate of a hometown friend. Fourteen. Yep, far too young to handle that kind of freedom. But I did. I handled it by being a "good girl." And I made up for the "good girl" thing by being better company, more fun, than most of the other girls. Again, my sense of humor saved me. I suppose some high school peers considered me "wild" because my friends were older, and I'd go to parties where there was drinking. I did smoke from the time I was thirteen. Sexually? I was a nun.

Once I came close to losing my virginity and didn't understand that it wasn't worthy of the shame I felt about it. In fact, it wasn't even my fault. Back then I was fairly certain I was responsible for everything.

An older cousin, a high school senior, beauty queen, and my idol, had something that might be today's equivalent of having one's own stadium skybox at seventeen: She had her own car. Sally would give me a ride home from school sometimes, after we stopped for a coke or a milkshake. She'd drive around for a while, sharing secrets she didn't confide to anyone else. I was barely fourteen, and any time spent with Sally was Nirvana.

Once when she had planned to give me a ride, Sally didn't show up. The bus had gone, and I was beginning to worry when her friend Brace appeared. Brace was a few years older than Sally, had finished school. He was a giant of a guy, Hulk-Hogan big. I didn't know him well, but she had told me Brace was like a brother. Their parents were friends, too.

Sally had called Brace from a pay phone on the way to Columbia and asked him to give me a ride home; she had needed to leave school early and didn't want me to be stranded.

I didn't give a second thought to jumping into Brace's shiny black convertible, a little disappointed the top wasn't down on such a warm, sunny day. He gave me a ride, yes he did, but not to my house. He drove down a red clay road where there were no houses. Since it hadn't rained for a while, his car was stirring up red dust. He stopped, and I thought something was wrong with the car. When I asked, he pulled me over to him real fast. His hands were big as baseball gloves.

Before I could take it all in, his tongue was in my mouth, pushing toward my throat; I was afraid I'd throw up. Couldn't breathe. I struggled, but he didn't let go. One huge hand went under my skirt. Stunned wouldn't be a strong enough word. Shattered? Closer.

Somehow I was able to wrench away enough to speak, "Brace, what are you—" About then his other hand went down my blouse, twisting a nipple; it hurt. I tried pushing his hand away, but he was strong. He moved the hand from under my skirt, using it instead to immobilize my free arm. "Stop it!" I screamed.

When he wouldn't stop, I burst into tears and began sobbing, scared and ashamed. I'm pretty sure my sobs were the reason he finally shoved me to the other end of the car seat. Now I was an offensive object he wanted out of his way. He seemed angry, and I didn't understand why. What had I done? I wasn't a flirtatious girl. I didn't even know how to flirt. What had I done to cause this?

After pushing me away, he started the car, screeching tires making clouds of red dust. I don't remember anything about the drive home. Had he thought I was an easy girl? How could he be like a brother to Sally and do what he had just done? Had he ever done that to her? Somehow I didn't think so, or surely she wouldn't be his friend.

I would hash out the Brace experience, and some similar, far worse, issues, in therapy years later. I'm astounded that I feel so shaky writing about him now, after all these years. I don't remember whether he threatened me about telling Sally or anyone else, can only guess that he might have. But I didn't tell her and probably wouldn't have, even without being threatened. I didn't tell anyone because the experience had made me feel dirty. Ashamed. I kept thinking I must have done *something* for him to think he could put his hands on me that way and put his tongue in my mouth. If I told Sally, it would ruin their friendship and it meant a lot to her. I was all about protecting her, even protecting him. I was protective of everyone in my life.

I never was a child? Yes, I was. It just worked out better for everybody else if I didn't act like one.

***

I was excited about majoring in journalism at the University, but a few days before registration my parents talked me into a two-year business course instead. That way I could work in an office if, heaven forbid, something happened to my future husband. "If something happened" was code for "if he dies." Divorce wasn't thought about much then, and mortality wasn't mentioned in any situation. There was certainly no thought that I might never marry. It was much later that I realized "learning to type" was about my mother's fear rather than her lack of faith in my ability to succeed in more demanding studies. To her mind she was empowering rather than limiting me. A lot was taken for granted then. It was 1962.

Not quite eighteen, I moved into a freshman dorm at the University of South Carolina on a suffocating August day. The rooms weren't air conditioned. I registered for classes in a two-year business program that included typing, shorthand, and office management. Electives in the English Department were as close as I got to journalism.

Since my classes weren't challenging there was time to make friends, play bridge, and dance in shiny "weejun" loafers until my feet sprouted blisters. I also wrote a weekly column for *The Gamecock,* the USC newspaper. My solemn, studious roommate once threw a shoe at me in frustration. It damn near made her crazy that I didn't have to struggle to get good grades the way she did. She couldn't understand there's not a lot of studying involved with typing, shorthand, and office machines. You either knew it or you didn't.

I ran for a freshman seat on the University's Student Senate and, to my amazement, I won. Having grown up with politics, I knew something about campaigning. I had become a political activist at age six, greeting voters at the polls when Papa ran for the House, then the Senate. I had met mill shifts with him and stuffed campaign flyers into mailboxes and screen doors.

I had good grades that weren't hard to get both semesters. One or two electives did require some book-cracking for exams, but I actually enjoyed having to study some.

At the end of freshman year at USC, I was introduced to a man I'll call "Ben" at a party in my home town. The people there were mostly couples my parents' age. In fact, I'm fairly sure I was there with my parents. Ben was the new golf pro at the country club, good looking. Maybe because I was single and no doubt the youngest person there, he seemed glad to spend time talking with me. It was obvious he was older, and I saw him as a man of the world. He had a funny way of turning his head all the way around to look at something or someone. It was an affectation I associated with being stuck-up. Only later did I learn it was more affliction than affectation. He had lost an eye in an automobile accident and was wearing a prosthesis. He had to turn his head to see.

A few days later Ben invited me to Columbia for dinner and a movie. It was early June, and we began seeing each other regularly. He enjoyed spending time with my parents, sharing a love of sports, especially golf and football, with my father. We spent evenings at my parents' house, having drinks on the screened porch. And sometimes, when he got home early enough, Papa would grill steaks. We'd go to Club functions with my parents or out to eat at the local Moose Lodge or someplace more upscale in Columbia. I was double-dating and having cocktails with my parents at eighteen! Ben hadn't made friends in town yet, other than Club members, so my parents and their friends were generally the people we continued to spend time with. They were good company, and I was mindful that there's safety in numbers.

Ben was twenty-seven, and I was eighteen at the time. While we were dating that summer, I kept in mind that all it would take to "kill" my mother and grandmother was for me to give in to Ben's insistent declarations that he "wanted" me.

Before long, Ben told me he loved me. Then, after saying and doing everything he could come up with to get me to capitulate, he finally played his winning card. He gave me an ultimatum that went something like this: College boys might be satisfied holding hands at the movies and necking in the car, but that wasn't enough for a man like himself. He loved me, he said, but if I didn't love him enough to take care of his needs, he'd be gone. It took me a long time to realize how young eighteen really was.

If I gave over the golden idol of virginity, there was no choice. I told myself we'd be getting married. I convinced myself it would be okay to sleep with him once we were officially engaged, and by summer's end he had given me a ring. Even before the fact I felt lousy about it, ashamed. What if he felt contempt afterwards? Brace had pushed me away in disgust, and we hadn't even "done it."

As it turned out, my beloved was too busy whistling to consider pushing me away. And me? Well, it wasn't anything like the movies. Not like the movies at all.

In September I returned to school for the second year, and after a month I was dealing with a kidney infection. It was rough; high fever and a reaction to the medication that made me even sicker. Bottom line, I wouldn't be able to complete the semester, so I went home. Ben and I decided to marry in February rather than waiting until summer. Once the kidney problem was resolved, I took a clerical job in Columbia and began planning the wedding.

Sidebar: I didn't have a car of my own, not even after I was married. While saving for one, I shared gas expenses and commuted with a cranky woman with a job in the same building. She would complain all the way up and down that 35-mile road to Columbia. She'd either talk about her gall bladder or other equally unpleasant topics in her grab-bag of negativity.

After day one, I turned on the high-beam optimism and made it my business to light up her life. It wasn't a totally successful undertaking, but over time she did relax a little and griped a bit less. The turning point came when I convinced this puritanical, blue-haired widow to stop at a convenience store about halfway home. I insisted on treating her to "the coldest beer in South Carolina," and, yep, it was legal to have an open container in the car in the 60's. The brew seemed to cheer her up, so we revisited that pit stop often. The store owner would put each icy-cold can in a little brown paper bag, carefully rolled down at the top.

Gladys pretty much sucked all the good energy out of me five days a week. Even worse, she made it impossible for me to feel anything like TV's single working girl, Mary Tyler Moore. Today I call people like "Glad-ass" energy vampires and run as fast as I can in the opposite direction when I see them coming. I have excellent energy-vampire radar now, and it stays activated.

***

When I got into bed two nights before our winter wedding, I dissolved in tears. I was more than tired; it had been a stressful couple of months. Even good times can be stressful. I had worked until the day before and had been honored at parties on weekends and some weeknights. But I know now, with certainty, that stress and exhaustion weren't the only factors. I had a "knowing," one of those warnings I learned to heed later. Back then I had no clue. My mother came into the room and sat on my bed. She was worried and obviously uncomfortable, telling me I was okay; brides have been known to fall apart before the wedding. She pointed out it was a good thing my tears were happening now because my eyes wouldn't be all puffy for the wedding.

I don't remember everything we said to each other. I told her, more or less, that I was afraid I might be making a mistake. She said that was perfectly normal, not to worry. I do know what wasn't said. I believe that, in her mind, there was no way out at this point, even if I had been sure what I wanted. And I wasn't sure at all. So, I went along with her assessment that I was simply experiencing a case of pre-nuptial nerves.

The invitations said we'd be married at five o'clock on Saturday, February 8. Mother and I forgot to include the year. People figured out what year we meant though, because the church parking lot was overflowing, and cars lined the street for blocks. The black limo moved toward the ceremony like a tranquilized turtle, trying to time it just right, I suppose. I remember sitting in the back seat of that funeral home car with my white dress fanned out around me like a cloud. In the front seat Papa talked college basketball with the thin-lipped undertaker. The irony of arriving in a vehicle of death at the place where I would begin my new life was lost on me at the time. We sat in that car in front of the church for what seemed like forever. I heard what is said to be the oldest striking Town Clock in the United States of America strike five.

Miss Caroline, a family friend, was acting as wedding director. She stood by the limo like a member of the palace guard. She did gesture now and then through the rolled-up window, making little ghosts with her breath in the cold twilight. I realized later she was trying to keep me calm. By ten after five, I was worried about Ben. An accident or some equally terrible thing must have happened to cause him to be late. It hadn't occurred to me that when my groom finally arrived, he would be a little wobbly in his tux. He had been drinking on the golf course with his father and brother all afternoon. We made it through the brief ceremony, but during the recessional he stopped to chat with his mother about a cousin of theirs. They actually had a conversation while I stood beside him in the aisle, the wedding party waiting behind us. I was mortified.

During the reception, Ben drank champagne. He had reserved the honeymoon suite at a motel in Augusta, so he wasn't willing to stay in Columbia on our wedding night. Looking back, it's amazing I wasn't furious with him. But I wasn't in touch with my emotions then, couldn't identify what I was feeling. I only thought *this isn't how it's supposed to be;* mostly, I was embarrassed that he was presenting himself in that state to our friends and relatives. I wanted them to know the Ben I was proud to be in love with, not see him the way he was that night. I was totally dejected, but pretending to be fine, on what supposedly was "the happiest day of my life."

A friend drove us as far as Columbia in my new husband's car, with her husband following in theirs. I was all dressed up in my going-away outfit, wearing a corsage lifted from the bouquet. It was an off-white wool suit, the Jackie Kennedy look, and I wore a hot-pink hat with a silk rose on it. I don't think I was fully aware of changing clothes or tossing the bouquet or running through the gauntlet of rice. In the car, I rode up front while my man was conked out in the back seat. I didn't know what to do. I did know he wouldn't be in any shape to drive when we got to Columbia in less than an hour, and I didn't want to drive on a dark, unfamiliar highway to our honeymoon suite. I didn't realize until we arrived in Columbia that I'd been clutching the traditional box of reception food like a life raft. A special bottle of champagne to have at the hotel was wedged between my aching feet.

Ben wouldn't be talked out of Augusta, so I drove while he nodded off in the passenger seat, waking with a clueless grin from time to time. I was terrified of hitting a deer or a patch of ice. I woke him to get directions to the hotel; amazingly, he was able to direct me and then get our key from the office. It was a cinderblock motel, and the room smelled musty and sour. I suppose a king-size bed made the "honeymoon" part legit, but there was no living area to make it a suite. Ben opened the champagne while I went into the bathroom to change into my wedding-night gown. I could hear him snoring even before I came out.

I remember sitting up in bed with a glass of champagne, pinching off bites of wedding cake and feeling numb. I talked myself out of crying. Wouldn't want Ben to feel bad about spoiling our wedding if he should wake up and find me in tears. And of course I didn't want to begin my first day as a married woman with red, swollen eyes.

Mammy would have been proud that Ben "hadn't touched me" on our wedding night. It would mean I had married a gentleman.

***

Recently I unearthed a journal that reminded how much I loved my husband. The man I married was honest and likable. He had a sense of humor, and people warmed to him easily.

I understood much later was that I had unrealistic expectations of him and of what our marriage would look like. I believed, because he was older and had more life experience, that he also would be wiser, stronger, and fearless. I idealized him. In reality, he turned out to be merely human, no stronger or wiser or more mature or less afraid than I. Yes, I was disappointed, but I didn't stop loving him, or trying mightily to please him.

I had no clue who I was then. Didn't know I was supposed to be a self-actualized person. I had no idea what my preferences were in home furnishings, clothes or far more significant things. I generally wore the same styles as my mother; in fact, we often shared clothes. Mostly, she shared hers because hers were far nicer. Our color scheme and furniture were much like my parents' furnishings. Any boundary between my mother and me was blurred at best. It never occurred to me that I could do things differently. That I *am* different.

As I said earlier, I couldn't identify what I was feeling then. I was navigating blindly through the marriage and through life, often behaving like a martyr, deferring to his preferences. I'm sure that the word "bitch" would have applied at times when I was feeling especially insignificant to Ben.

I not only knocked myself out attempting to please him, but my lifelong compulsion to anticipate the needs of others and my own need to win approval, were operating in overdrive. Efforts to "make him happy" caused me to dumb down a lot, too. When we argued, he would say, "You think you're so smart." It had more to do with Ben's self image than with me. But I didn't realize it then. I had never thought of myself as especially bright. In fact, I felt "slow" in some respects because I have what probably is a form of ADHD. I don't think people were tested for that when I was growing up, or maybe my parents didn't notice I was struggling. I did read a lot though, and you can't help learning things if you're a reader. Once into therapy, I was able to recognize and own my intelligence more and more.

Over the years Ben never was physically abusive, and I never knew him to be unfaithful. Sure, he had flaws, and so did I. We rarely argued during those first few years, partly because we agreed on most things—life in general, politics, friends. And partly because of my people-pleasing tendencies and Ben's easy-going manner. Probably the main bone of contention was his not calling when he'd be late coming home. When Ben was very late, my first thought would be of him laid out in a hospital morgue or trapped and bleeding in his mutilated Chevrolet. I'd vacillate between fear and anger, then get around to feeling unloved and disrespected. And back to fear again until he finally came home.

I always wanted someone, especially Ben, to worry about me every now and then, to be concerned for my safety and well-being. Once I was late getting home from work in Columbia and shaken when I got there. Ben was watching TV. When I asked whether he'd been worried about me, he said, absently, "No, I know you can take care of yourself." I had been in an accident and unable to reach him. No cell phones then.

***

We lived the first eighteen months in a renovated barn in an elderly cousin's back yard. Rent was $40 a month, so our modest small-town living expenses made my commuting to work with Gladys worthwhile. After Ben accepted a club pro's job in Columbia, we both commuted for about six months before giving up our cozy nest. And the low rent.

The Barn was rustic, whitewashed outside, paneled inside; there was even a white picket fence. A window seat, and built-in bookshelves on either side of the windows, added to the charm in the rectangular living-eating space. That was in the center, and the master bedroom was on the left of the front door when you walked in. A laughably small guest room, bath, and kitchen were on the right. Apparently our bedroom had been used for horse stalls, with the dividers removed. The kitchen was cramped and outdated, but I didn't mind. I could just as well open a can of English peas, cover baking potatoes in foil and broil a package of frozen fish there as anywhere else and be proud to serve it to any dinner guest during those blissful years of being a young and ignorant hostess.

One weekend a longtime friend of Ben's came to visit at The Barn. His girlfriend recently had refused his marriage proposal. After a late dinner of Ben's grilled steaks, I decided to call it a night, give the two of them some time together.

While reading in bed, I felt a mule-kick to the belly when I overheard the love of my life saying, "You know, I wasn't in love with her. Just decided it was time to settle down. I mean, she's a sweet girl, pretty, and she does love my ass!" They laughed before Ben continued. "There's some girl out there who will love your ass enough to marry you, too, buddy." A couple of days later I found the courage to tell him what I'd overheard. He tried to convince me he was just saying that to cheer up his friend. I knew better, and he knew I knew better, but I didn't know what I'd do if I accepted the truth. So, I put it out of my mind and made it my business to get him to love me. A familiar endeavor.

Several years later we were at Ben's parents' on Christmas night. At some point when another couple started to bicker, Ben said, "The difference between you two and us is that you love each other, but you don't like each other; we like each other, but we don't love each other." This time I was in the room. I don't know what happened after that. Maybe some merciful soul made me a loaded eggnog. It seemed to be a simple statement of fact. I didn't make a fuss, nor did anyone else. It was Christmas, after all.

***

Sidebar: We had joked about staying at The Barn until after we had a child. That was because, when our little one left a door open one day, someone might ask the question so popular in the South, "Were you raised in a barn?" We imagined our child answering that indeed he was raised in a barn. Thinking about that would crack us up. Without the ability to laugh, I don't think we'd have made it.

Our son wasn't raised in a barn, though. We moved to Columbia before he was even conceived.

***

I will share passages from the journal I rediscovered recently, about twenty pages in a spiral notebook. Some entries are related to our son Neal's birth—lists of visitors and gifts received, with check marks indicating I'd written a proper thank you note. I was astounded to see what a tough task-master I was to myself.

The journal confirmed that I didn't know how to ask for what I needed or wanted then. It was obvious I wasn't able to acknowledge, or even recognize, anger. These entries are from 1967, not long before our son was born. Seeing the young woman I was then with "new eyes" I felt a little embarrassed for her, and sad. There was also tenderness for the younger version of myself. More significantly, the journal gave me a clear perspective on my personal growth since that time.

March 3, 1967

... Three years ago my name was changed to the name of the best man in the world, the most thoroughly good person in my life who actually IS my life. I so adore him!

We celebrated our third anniversary on February 8, and my most complete happiness began with the first movements of the baby we're expecting in May. We are settled in our very own home now. Our marriage has taken on a whole new world of meaning. We painted all six rooms of the house ourselves before moving in, and never have I washed so many windows ... had my first experience at floor waxing, hands and knees style!

April 3, 1967

Am almost ashamed to write the date, since it has been a month ere I wrote last. [ere?!] Now I feel the urge to complain, and these pages will seem sympathetic. I only hope that my unburdening will be satisfied before Ben gets home.

The day is a beautiful one. Our entire neighborhood is a wonderland with azaleas and dogwood in bloom. As usual, I have kept busy enough and should be content with some quiet time for rest. Instead, I've allowed myself at the twilight hour to become frustrated and very nearly depressed.

Somehow, some way, from the outset of our courtship and marriage I believe I adjusted to the damnable hours a golf pro must keep. I learned to take holidays as "just another day" and the same goes for weekends, a pro's busiest time. By the end of a lengthening spring or summer day, I am usually standing at the door waiting with a kiss. Naturally on his day off, Ben plays golf, as rightly he should. He loves the game and after watching others go out to play all week, it's only fair for him to have some fun. I suppose it's the approaching daylight savings time that has me at a low tolerance level. He will be getting home at 9 rather than 8, and that's a long day for anybody. Besides hating it for his sake, it's only natural (I hope), and maybe somewhat selfish, to think about how it's going to affect our life together, especially with the approaching birth of our baby.

I hope venting my feelings here will help me cope with myself more effectively ....

Really, diary, there have been so many happy and rewarding days since I wrote last. I'm sorry to pick a bad time to record my feelings. [Present-day note: It's hard looking at my martyrdom here, and I can't believe I'm apologizing to a freaking diary!]

April 4 1967

Should truly apologize [again!] for letting off so much steam last night, but it helped. The evening turned out fine. During the night I had scary stomach pains and didn't sleep much. Was glad when daylight came, and Ben got up to go to the Masters. I hope thinking about my pains won't ruin his day in Augusta. Somehow I can't hide my fears from him, and it would be counted as my greatest feat if only I could learn to.

May 3, 1967

Daylight savings time went into effect April 30, and I loathe it. It's nearly 9 o'clock and Ben still isn't home. How I do miss him! And I know the poor darling will come home exhausted.

Notes on revisiting the journal: This revelation, sometime after recording all that, underscored how naive I was at the time. Ben often opted to play golf, visit with buddies in the pro shop, or have drinks in the bar at the end of his work day. It was not often the demands of the job that kept him late. I suppose turning him into something of a martyr in my mind helped me avoid seeing that not coming home earlier was his choice. And it kept me from having to admit to myself that I was second choice at best.

Not least, I was glad to be reminded in my own words how much I did love and "adore" my husband. It was sad to see how I denied my own wants and needs, though, how I turned myself inside out to be cheerful. How determined I was not to be a burden to him or anyone else. Maybe I sensed the high risk that he might leave the marriage.

***

After Neal arrived we couldn't have been happier. "Planet Neal" was where I lived, a place of deeper feelings; there was a fierce, but tender, unconditional love I never knew before or since. He gave my life a whole new purpose.

I was comfortable with him from the minute the nurse put him in my arms. I had thought I'd be nervous holding my tiny newborn. Ben was relaxed with him, too, even changed diapers which, believe it or not, was not the norm at that time.

For the first twenty-two months of Neal's life, I was able to be at home with him. It was a good time. But there were some financial potholes in the road, and it became necessary for me to return to work. It was hard to accept the reality of Neal being at a child care center five days a week. I didn't want to miss hearing even one new word or seeing one new expression. But it was one of the times I needed to work, like it or not.

***

Our marriage ran for several years on the sweet fumes of family life. Ben and I were optimists, and we wanted our son to have a happy childhood.

It mattered to me that we share most evening meals, something that rarely happened when I was growing up. Weekdays, after collecting Neal from day care, I'd spend a little time with him before settling him in to watch a new TV show he loved, *Sesame Street* I'd head to the kitchen, putting together a meal of meat and vegetables, or something simple like soup or chili with salad with cornbread. No microwave. My repertoire had expanded a little since the frozen-fish-and-canned-peas days at the Barn. When Neal was four or five, I did "theme meals" from other countries once a week; using a globe as a centerpiece along with whatever props I could come up with. It was a short-lived tradition, but fun while it lasted.

Sadly, the fumes of family living weren't enough to sustain the marriage. Ben was out later more often, and he was less and less engaged when he was at home. The more detached he became, the more I urged him to share what was going on with him which, of course, exacerbated the situation. He'd provoke arguments about nonsensical things, sometimes ending with a walk-out or declaring "I don't know why you want to stay married to me."

A couple of years after Neal was born, Ben left his golf pro job. He took a straight commission situation working with a friend. That didn't turn out as well as he'd hoped, but after a time Ben was hired as an account rep at a local TV station. There was a good salary with benefits and, best of all, regular hours. He liked the work, and I thought I'd be able to stay home with Neal again soon, before he started school. But after a short while Ben became dissatisfied with the job and resigned. I was heartsick over what I saw as a big mistake, but it was a done deal, so I did my best to accept the situation.

It was around that time I began to realize Ben wanted out of the marriage, and he was hoping I'd be the one to leave. He wouldn't even talk about counseling. Since I had no intention of giving up, one night he finally said that he wanted out. Even though his announcement shouldn't have come as a shock, it did. Maybe I was in some form of denial for the months leading up to it. But I still loved him or was convinced I did. Even now I'm not sure which it was. I suppose I kept hoping Ben would change his mind and agree to our getting some professional help.

***

Neal and I moved to an apartment complex next door to a city park where he would later play Little League and take karate classes. He was almost six when we separated. Ben handled the sale of our house. We took a loss, and Ben soon took a job in Florida.

The first night at the apartment was the first in my adult life I had been without the presence of another adult overnight. Besides being in a state of grief, I was afraid. Really scared. And more than whatever I was afraid might "get" us, I didn't want Neal to sense my fear. I didn't want him to grow up fearful. My dream of a carefree childhood for him went out the window with the family breakup. Now, more than ever, I wanted him to feel secure and protected. That first night, when Neal was sleeping, I shoved a desk in front of the apartment door. Neal was a heavy sleeper, so I didn't need to worry about repositioning the desk until time to wake him the next morning. The barricade became a nightly ritual.

Neal had a hard time with the disappearance of his familiar life in a two-parent family. Before moving to Florida, Ben had seen Neal regularly, and now Neal was missing his dad. He began to act out with temper tantrums, and I knew we both needed help. I remain grateful to the psychological social worker who had the skills to get through to my six-year-old son. He couldn't change our situation or make Neal's loss okay, but he did help Neal see what I couldn't; that this separation wasn't his fault, and he always would be loved by both parents. While he met with his counselor, I saw a psychologist down the hall. With her, I began to understand that I had a lot of healing to do, and I began to believe that healing was possible. I made some progress, but it wasn't until years later that I worked with a therapist who would help me go deeper.

I surprised Neal with a guitar for his seventh birthday and hired a college student to teach him to play it. He loved the guitar, and he was crazy about Debbie. He was hooked on making music. Now, as an adult, he plays at his church and professionally when time allows. He has a wonderful voice and writes some of his own songs. Unbiased entertainment reviewers have agreed with his mother's opinion.

My father handled the simple, "amicable" divorce. It was simple, but not without pain. It was simple because there were no significant assets involved. Thanks to my generous father, neither Ben nor I had the burden of attorney fees. Neal and I lived in the apartment for three years, and it got easier being without Ben. Easier for me, at any rate.

***

About two years later Ben became head pro at a club in Texas. Neal visited him that summer. During Neal's visit, Ben and I had phone conversations ranging from cordial to friendly to familiar. I flew out there to help celebrate his fortieth birthday and bring Neal back to South Carolina. I wanted to be sure he *came* back. I missed him.

Our son, our common cause, liked being in Texas. He had made friends and was playing some golf with his dad. Ben seemed happy in his job. Dissatisfaction with his work had been a problem in the past, and that had been hard on our marriage. It was good to see him feeling good about himself and his life. He was doing well, except about the fact that Neal would be leaving in a few days.

It's astonishing to think about now, but back then it was all too easy to lapse into my default pattern: assessing the needs and wants of the people in my life, then doing whatever it took to see that their needs were met, their wishes fulfilled. I tended to ignore my own, especially if they might interfere with the wishes of anyone else. I was not only a martyr but a fairy godmother-martyr.

At some point I said "yes" to Ben's less-than-romantic entreaty, "We get along better than most couples I know; why don't we get married again?" He had met me at the airport with flowers. *That* was romantic, and he volunteered to spend time off exploring the area with me once we were married. We'd have fun. I'd see. We both pretended it wasn't all about Neal, but I knew. And Ben knew it was the only way to have Neal there with him. I wasn't quite as naive then as I had been at nineteen, but I was still as co-dependent.

I flew back to South Carolina to make the announcement to family and friends and have our belongings moved to the Lone Star State. Neal stayed behind with his dad. It was hard dealing with some of the shock waves when I told people my plans, and it was painful saying goodbye. I'd never lived away from family and friends. They were a huge part of my life, my identity. It was nearly impossible to think of living so far from my mother. She was stoic about the news, happy for Neal, and promised to visit soon.

I packed everything we owned and saw that it was loaded on the moving van. Years later Mama said that watching the moving van pull away was the saddest moment in her life.

***

Holding on to the image of Neal's happy face, I returned to Texas and Ben's flooded apartment. I squish-squashed through my new reality for a couple of weeks until we moved to a bigger, drier apartment. Not a minute too soon. I was nearing wit's end, compounding misery with false bravado.

On the first day of new-apartment access, I discovered it hadn't been cleaned. It never occurred to me to complain or that I'd be justified if I did. This time I wasn't the child bride romanticizing the floor-scrubbing, but an exhausted woman running low on optimism. Finding a pubic hair in the refrigerator finally broke me. The floodgates opened. I remember sitting on the just-cleaned kitchen floor, letting out gut-wrenching sobs. When I thought about picking Neal up at school, I sat up straight, panicked about my swollen, red eyes. I didn't want my son to see that his mama was miserable. My sunglasses weren't rose-colored, but they served the purpose that day.

***

Ben had made it clear, when he presented the marriage idea, that he didn't want me to work. That suited me. I had slogged through office jobs for years, most days trying to stay positive about my work situation. We had needed my group health insurance. In Texas we all would be covered through Ben's job.

Looking back, our time in Texas might have been less lonely if I had worked, maybe part-time. But it wouldn't have fixed things. I felt certain that my not working was connected to Ben's self-esteem, and I wouldn't have wanted to rock that boat.

We had the marriage license and only needed to get down to the courthouse for the judge to finalize our reunion. Ben called one morning to say he'd swing by the apartment in twenty minutes to pick me up. He was bringing the license.

I changed clothes and freshened my makeup. I needn't have bothered. We sat on a grimy bench at the courthouse in a hallway where people were waiting to visit relatives in jail. One woman was nursing her baby, and the couple sitting across from us seemed on the verge of fighting. I tried not to stare. The hallway was gloomy, not a single redeeming feature about the place, aesthetically speaking.

I sipped on a Mountain Dew while Ben and I made small talk. As we waited, the theme from "Love Story" was not playing in my head. When a clerk called our names, they echoed in the corridor as we rose to meet the time-and-sun-weathered probate judge who would unite us in holy matrimony. Or maybe it was just matrimony since we weren't in a church. His Honor began reading from a book about the institution of marriage, and I realized, embarrassed, that I still was holding the bottle of Mountain Dew. I was glad Mammy wasn't there. If "a lady should never whistle in public," I was pretty sure a lady shouldn't hang on to a pop bottle during her wedding ceremony.

After our wedding— That is, after we got married, Ben dropped me off at the apartment. He had a golf match that afternoon. There was no celebration to mark the occasion, and the days clicked on by. I felt as if I'd been shot out of a cannon and landed on another planet. Actually, Texas is another planet. But that's another story.

***

The furniture arrived from South Carolina later that wedding week and I became absorbed in transforming a generic apartment into a home. It took some doing, but I needed a challenge. I hadn't begun to blossom creatively at the time, still didn't know what made my heart sing, and I'm sure I was concerned about how others might judge my efforts.

Our apartment home was traditional and comfortable, easy enough on the eyes; that's about the best I can say for it. I don't think it was tacky. I arranged my first art grouping over a sofa. The end result was nothing to jump up and down about, nothing to throw rocks at either. Nevertheless, I enjoyed having a taste of creative satisfaction.

Soon there was something to celebrate: my birthday. Ben was pretending he didn't remember. I guessed that he and Neal would surprise me with a gift and probably take me out for dinner. Actually, they didn't. They forgot. It was not the best year to forget, given I'd just uprooted myself from home and left behind everybody who would have celebrated me that day. This was before e-mail and unlimited long distance. I felt alone and insignificant once again. Cue the violins.

Even though I'd been away a whole month, I hadn't been forgotten back home. Cards, notes, and a check from my parents came in the mid-afternoon mail; there were some calls from "The Trinity," Emma, Mammy, and Mama , and a few friends. During the second call that night, Ben realized it was about my birthday. We went out for Mexican the next night. I didn't expect a store-bought gift from Neal, but I'd have loved a crayon drawing — maybe a house with big windows and a door, three stick figures, smoke curling up from a chimney, and of course an enormous sun radiating from a cloudless blue sky.

I thought about how our wedding day and my birthday went, then plugged my thoughts into gratitude. Although it meant having less time with Neal, it made me happy that he was nearly always doing something with his neighborhood buddies. They rode their bikes and congregated at the park just down the street or at one of their homes. Sometimes ours. He was happy; his childhood was turning into exactly what I'd wanted for him, a carefree time and a chance to grow up in a stable, healthy way. I was mindful that I shouldn't cling and risk turning him into a "Mama's boy." I did what I could to encourage his sensibilities without doing that.

Ben had painted a happy picture of exploring the area together on his days off. There were to be occasional overnight trips as well. But there was always some reason he couldn't get away, or there would be an out-of-town tournament. I soon gave up mentioning it. He seemed satisfied with things just as they were. Other than telling me something about a club member now and then, or repeating a joke he had heard, he shared next to nothing. He sometimes got testy when I showed interest and asked questions. We watched a lot of TV when we weren't doing something with Neal. I ironed Ben's golf shirts with great care and was conscientious about meals. He was complimentary about the meals. Nevertheless, I felt like a walk-on in our family play.

It was painfully obvious that I was still incidental to Ben. How could I have expected things to be different this time? There was little, if any, evidence of love coming my way. I was a means to an end, Neal being the end.

Ben worked with Neal to improve his golf swing and played with him. Sometimes I would ride in the cart, even hit some balls. Neal, at ten, occasionally helped out in the bag room at the Club. He liked being around an older cousin and the other high school kid who worked there. Ben or his assistant supervised the young workers.

Ben and Neal went camping at a local ranch with the neighborhood pals and their fathers. The camping pictures were a testament to happy times with flashlight duels and ghost stories around campfires. Sometimes they'd drive the seventy miles to San Antonio for Spurs games.

At some point Neal began acting out in class, mostly talking when he shouldn't, so I enrolled him in an acting class. If he wanted to be on stage, why not really be on stage? It felt good to be needed when I drove him out to the theater for classes or rehearsals. Those were special times together, longer than the rides home from school. Neal turned out to be a talented actor, enthusiastic about the classes and productions, and his school behavior improved.

***

With Neal at school and Ben at the club, I had free time most days, once the apartment was clean, laundry done, and the evening meal planned. Usually, I would write. I'd sit on the edge of our king-size bed, using a card table as a desk, and click away at my portable Smith Corona. At that time, mistakes had to be erased. Not easy, but easier than correcting some mistakes made in the course of living.

I not only wrote short stories and poems, I submitted some pretty bad stuff to some pretty good publications. I didn't know any better. Even with all the rejection slips, 72 in all, I soldiered on. Once when Joan Fontaine was in San Antonio doing dinner theater, I infuriated the theater's publicist by getting a phone interview on my own. I had approached the actress directly. I was a nervous wreck before making the call at the agreed time. Our dog, Pucci, was sequestered in Neal's bedroom with a TV and toys. I was hoping she wouldn't bark.

Ms. Fontaine was somewhat formal but pleasant, and I calmed down once we got started. From my research I knew she was a golfer, so I talked about the club where Ben worked to get things started. I asked about her favorite courses. I had read her book, *No Bed of Roses*, and everything I could read about her beforehand. Of course there was no computer for my research.

I wrote the article and sent her a copy before attempting to place it. I'm not sure that it ever was published, and I can't believe I don't remember that, important as it seemed at the time. I was thrilled when Ms. Fontaine called to say she couldn't remember reading anything so well-written, that many writers today are "not worth their salt ...." She had called a San Antonio editor to recommend me for a job with a daily paper there! The editor called me, said he might have something to talk about that summer. Neal and I would be going to South Carolina then, and I wasn't changing my plans. Besides, writing for a newspaper didn't interest me. And I hadn't forgotten that Ben didn't like the idea of my working.

Still, I appreciated Ms.Fontaine's affirmation. It was part of the reason I never stopped writing, except years later when I took a long time-out while working two full-time jobs, one for money and one for the nonprofit organization I started. Ms. Fontaine, along with the fact that I couldn't stop writing, kept me going. If you're a writer, you write. Whether it's good or not, whether you publish or not. The writing is inside you and it has to get out, like a puppy not allowed to pee on the carpet has to get out. There's simply no choice.

***

Neal's cousin Mac visited for ten days one summer. Ben took a day off then and came home early another day. We did it up big, took the boys to a rodeo with western dancing afterwards; *You picked a fine time to leave me Lucille* was playing at some point. We visited nearby towns and explored a crystal cave. The boys were enthusiastic about a nearby military museum where they climbed on a tank. Ben took the boys camping one night, and of course they spent time at the Club. I'm sure they ingested more than their share of chlorine in the pool.

A few of my friends visited, too, as did Ben's mother, my mother, and grandmother Mammy. When Mammy deplaned in San Antonio, she, who for years had disapproved of drinking, asked, "Have you ever heard of a wine called Bloody Mary?" She "didn't think much of it," she said, with eyes sparkling and her cheeks all pinked up. Mama and I exchanged winks and managed not to laugh.

***

Neal played junior basketball, and Ben and I would go to his games. It was nice doing that as a couple, as a family. Neal was thriving during that time. As far as school and activities went, I believe his time in Texas were his best years. High school wouldn't be such a carefree experience.

Neal and I would spend most of the summer in South Carolina with my parents, friends and their children. I took him to visit Ben's family, too. When we were in South Carolina, Neal especially loved having time with Mac and his older brother Paul. They were slightly older, but the three were close, as close to brothers as Neal had.

It was Ben's busiest season, and he was on the golf course every chance he got once Daylight Savings Time kicked in. That usually tamped down any guilt I had about being away for so long. South Carolina summers made the rest of the year bearable for me.

By the third year I was growing more and more despondent. I felt empty as a drum, and it became harder and harder to appear otherwise. I felt disconnected, like my soul was drying up, and my heart was heavy most of the time. It took a lot of energy pretending to others, indeed to myself, that all was well when I was screaming inside. It's unhealthy and irresponsible to live a lie, no matter how "noble" the reason. Living that way drains away life energy, leaving nothing in reserve. Once the life force is diminished, you can bet your number will be coming up for a disease, accident, or worse. I think some low-level depression was factoring in by then. Yet I kept trying to make it better, make it better, make it better. I felt purposeless and totally without support. Self-help books didn't help.

I missed the intimacy of friendship. How does that old song go? *Make new friends and keep the old, one is silver and the other gold.* I had been determined to bloom where I was planted, in this case the Texas caleche. So, I plotted the overthrow of loneliness and reached out.

My "silver" was three women who were amenable to friendship of a sort. Two of the three were alcoholics. One would call and talk at length. By the time I was able to get off the phone, her words would be unintelligible. The next day she rarely remembered we had talked. The other woman was really special, and I wish we could have enjoyed a close friendship at that time. But booze was her best friend, too, and she stayed busy with her own family dramas. Bottom line, she didn't have the capacity for a close friendship. The third woman who befriended me was having marital problems and often was verbally abusive to her daughters. It was painful to witness. After spending time with any of them, I'd feel drained and more alone than ever.

I remember treating myself to lunch at a Chinese restaurant in a strip mall, pulling into the parking lot feeling as if I were in another world. And indeed I was. It seemed surreal. I was becoming robotic, and the more robotic I became, the better I seemed to fit in. But I didn't want to be a robot.

People at the club, members and staff, were pleasant enough. Ben and I were included in the club's social events. But it all seemed so superficial, country club life and the conversations there. You can pretend to be interested in golf scores, tennis matches, and the Dallas Cowboys just so long. I didn't find anybody who seemed to care about what was going on in the larger world, meaning the world beyond the Texas State Line, or outside their own day-to-day experience. No one seemed to care about world affairs, the arts, or reading even popular fiction. Some of the members were outrageously wealthy; one woman sent their jet to California to pick up a special tablecloth from one of their homes, for a dinner party. Ben seemed to enjoy the country club banter, while I felt alone even in a big, rowdy crowd. I made sure to wear my smiling, socially-acceptable mask, and I knew better than to voice my political opinions.

Then one day I reached the end. It wasn't premeditated. There was just a sad awakening. That morning I did the breakfast dishes, ran the vacuum, and loaded clothes in the washer. I wrote a note to a friend and took it to the mailbox. Then, I sat at my card-table desk to write and thought, *Maybe I'll just add some brandy to this coffee.*

I poured a big glug of good brandy, then paused as I stirred. It was ten in the morning. What was I doing? I poured it down the sink. My misery wasn't going to lead me into addiction, because I wasn't going to allow it. I was about to live out Mary Oliver's poem, "The Journey," and I don't think it had been written at that time. When I read it some years later, it became my favorite poem. Anyone on the brink of making a hard decision or feeling fearful about making a needed life change would do well to read it. Absorb it.

Next morning I picked up boxes from stacks of empties outside a strip-mall. I wasn't consciously aware of why I was taking them. The boxes ended up in my closet, and soon I began filling them with books. I understood then that I would be going.

This part of the story is harder to tell. It was the beginning of a long struggle with pain and guilt. Gradually, over the next few years, the pain would diminish; the guilt would win out only when I'd forget I was saving my own life. I slowly began to hear and recognize my own voice. Over a longer period of time, those painful feelings have faded into a soft blanket of sadness that surrounds the Texas memories.

The opportunity to talk with Ben presented itself a few nights later when Neal was staying over at a friend's. When I told him I had to leave, had to go back home, he seemed puzzled. The main thing I remember about that night is his absolute determination that Neal would stay there with him. I'd never seen him that determined about anything, ever. He would fight me, he said. I hadn't considered the idea of going without Neal. There was more anguish than anger that night.

The exhaustion that comes after near-endless tears finally made way for some calm, reasoned discussion. Sad talk. Before the night was over, I had agreed that, for the coming school year, Neal would stay with him; we would be united on that. At twelve, Neal was doing well in school and still happy with his buddies. Ben never had needed to prove his manhood by being tough or pushing his son too hard; he knew how to nurture Neal when he was hurt or sick. And I took some small comfort in that.

I had no source of income and would have no place of my own once back in South Carolina. I recognized that I couldn't provide Neal with much stability if he were to go with me. He needed stability, and for now that would mean continuing his present living situation. I began to convince myself that he needed his father's masculine influence more than he needed me at this stage of his young life. But, mostly, I couldn't put him in the middle of a custody fight. He wasn't an object to be fought over. Still, the thought of being away from him affected me viscerally.

Ben and I agreed that, most of all, we needed to help Neal understand that we both loved him and our separating had nothing to do with him. None of our problems were his fault. He could count on us to pull together on his behalf.

Neal was heartbroken. He had heard all the words before. At one point he wrapped his arms around me, crying, "What if I want to go with you?" And, I wanted to say "You do? Then you can!" Instead, I said the hardest, kindest thing I could say: "Honey, this doesn't get to be your decision. This was a hard grownups' decision. You know your Dad and I decided it's best for you to stay here for the school year. You and I can talk on the phone any time you want; before we know it, you'll be coming to South Carolina for a long visit." I don't know how I got those words out. They felt brutal.

In the weeks that remained, living together with the inevitable parting on the horizon was hard. Ben alternated between anger and behaving as though nothing had changed. The mother of a friend of Neal's tried to shame me and succeeded. But she didn't change my mind. When you're engulfed in flames, you can't be shamed off the fire escape.

The truth, or as much of the truth as I can put into words, is this: I could have fought to have Neal come with me, and I probably would have won for two reasons. It was pretty much established precedent at the time that minor children remained with the mother unless the mother could be proven unfit. I had lawyers, good ones, among family and friends. But the person who would have lost, been hurt most in a battle like that, would have been Neal. So I had surrendered. There was no turning back.

***

I sent Brother a plane ticket. He would fly out, visit a few days, then help me drive back to South Carolina. Hard to believe now that, in addition to preparing to leave and all that entailed, I was willing to remain in my emotional quagmire an extra three days. Why? Because I wanted Brother to enjoy himself! He had come all the way out there for me, after all. Southern hospitality still trumped damn near everything.

Ben, Neal, and I took Brother out for Texas-style country fried steak with that awful white gravy, and we had Mexican food one night. Ben arranged for us to visit club members, hotshot gun lovers who hunted big game from their private plane. Brother just had to see the stuffed polar bear and all the other amazing (appalling) animals these people had killed and now used as home decor. Elephant feet had become bases for tables with glass tops. Brown bears were stuffed so their paws could hold trays of party food. Zebra rugs, lions, tigers, and bears, oh boy. I'm serious. *These are not my people,* I was thinking as the host offered us a cocktail.

Actually, the four of us had a pretty good time while Brother was there. I believe that made the departure seem all the more bizarre and ultimately harder for everybody.

The morning Brother and I were leaving, my exorcist green Dodge Charger was packed and ready to go. A few things, including my father's century-old Senate desk, would be sent as an add-on load when a truck was heading my way. I was fighting tears and waving goodbye after peeling myself away from Neal. As Brother pulled away from the curb, I turned to him and said, "Let's get the Dodge out of Hell."

There wasn't a mother alive who could have felt any worse that day or in the days ahead. As soon as we turned the corner, I broke down. Pretty much cried all the way to Louisiana, much to Brother's chagrin. That was the end of a major chapter, I suppose, but not the end of the story.

***

Once back in South Carolina I lived under an avalanche of emotional conflict: grief, exhaustion, relief, and the beginnings of hope for the future, whatever it might hold. It would be nearly two years before I'd find a therapist who could help me identify, for the first time in my life, what I was feeling. I was struggling not to show the nearly paralyzing pain of being separated from Neal. We talked regularly, and he seemed to be doing well. I'd tell myself it was selfish to long for the sight of him, to want to see in his eyes that he was really okay. After all, I was to blame for the fact that we were living in different states. Wasn't I?

Sidebar: Looking back, I can see how harshly I judged my decision to leave the marriage. I felt the sting of judgment from others, too. Even with a few friends, the unspoken question was there: "How could you do it?" I asked myself "how" many times and never got an answer. There's no guilt quite like maternal guilt. But I do know "why" I left. I needed to save my life after the soul-smothering time in Texas.

Even with that understanding, I know my decision affected Neal's life profoundly. It's always there between us, showing itself like a Dickens' ghost of Christmas past when I least expect it.

I'm lucky to have a perceptive, candid friend who helps me stay honest with myself. She has played a big part in my healing and growth for years. After reading this chapter, she pointed out that I'm still taking on the blame and feeling guilt for leaving the second marriage, and especially for allowing Neal to stay with Ben. She reminded me that Ben had left the first marriage, which also meant leaving Neal. And he had not lived up to his promises in the second one. She also thought it took a lot of courage to risk marrying Ben the second time. I know in my head that what she says is true. And after all this time, my heart is beginning to believe it, too.

***

I was staying with my parents. They weren't emotionally equipped to witness, much less talk about, my feelings surrounding the Texas leave-taking. But they made me feel welcome, insisting I stay as long as I wanted. Neal would join me for the Christmas holidays and summer.

I signed on with an employment agency, getting a few temporary assignments, office jobs, until I could find something permanent. What was to be my last agency obligation was at a behemoth law firm in downtown Columbia. The experience was like none I'd had before. I was somewhat familiar with legal work, having filled in for my father's secretary when she was on vacation or when things got backed up at his office. But, fine trial attorney that he was, Papa was a self-defined "country lawyer." His pace was hardly breakneck, and he wasn't all about the money. The term "billable hours" wasn't familiar to him. In later years he would deplore the shift in his profession's primary emphasis; he felt it had gone from championing the client to how much money the client's case would generate.

Yes, this firm was very different from my father's one-man practice. With all the prestige and paneled impeccability of the partners' offices, you might never notice that the place was a sweat shop. Remember the classic "*I Love Lucy*" episode where Lucy and Ethel are working in the candy factory? They can't keep up with production as the conveyor belt moves faster and faster; they're in a race with impossibility, stuffing candy everywhere. Hilarious schtick.

In this situation I was Lucy minus Ethel, and there was nothing funny about it. Instead of candy coming at me too fast, files were dumped on my assigned desk every few minutes, often without instructions about what I should do with them. At one point I had the idea that one of my friends might have planned an elaborate practical joke.

Even though I was an excellent typist and had barely looked up all day, the stack of files kept getting taller. To top it off, I was treated either as invisible or like Cinderella by attorneys and the step-sister staff. My assignment was for a week, possibly longer. I had a strong work ethic and, back then, a need to do everything perfectly. Consequently, my first day ended in despair as I stared at a Tower of Pisa made of legal files.

The second day I was at the law office early and dug in before I could even clock in. By noon, anxiety had set up shop in my solar plexus. There was no way I could meet these people's expectations. It just wasn't going to happen. My hyper-responsibility was at war with reason, and I was beginning to panic when creativity came to the rescue.

I went into the women's room and washed off my makeup. I didn't have the skills then to address the situation with the employment agency, and I couldn't afford to have a bad record there. Even then, white lies weren't in my repertoire. At the same time, we can only meet ourselves where we are and work with what we have in a crisis. Sometimes our standards may be too high to resolve an impossible situation.

I was on the Titanic here, and I latched on to the only lifeboat within reach: I lied. Pretended to be sick. Apparently, a stomach virus had been the right idea. It seemed to have a fear factor of, say, leprosy. Before I could sling my handbag over my shoulder, they were showing me the door and whipping out the Lysol.

On the elevator going down to the lobby, I was repeating my own version of the Scarlet O'Hara with the turnip mantra: "As God is my witness, I'll never work at a law firm again." And I didn't. Work at a law firm or go hungry.

***

My friend Suzanne was planning to supplement her teaching income with a brand-new real estate license when she suggested that my father buy a residential property in Columbia. She knew just the one. Maybe Brother and I could rent it from him until we were each able to buy our own places; my father still would have it as an investment. Since it was in one of the few remaining downtown neighborhoods, property value was destined to go up, she said. My generous father accepted her idea, and that's how Brother and I became next-door neighbors in an old, cosmetically-refurbished mill village duplex.

The working cotton mill was about a quarter of a block across the street, in full view. Directly opposite our duplex were two houses. One was owned and occupied by the Snell family. They shopped flea markets and loaded up their front porch, and sometimes the yard, with their excellent finds. I was half scared of mama-bear Snell until I visited one day and bought one of her flea market treasures. It was an old wooden ballot box with frosted glass around the sides and a slot in the top. I would use it as a side table. Mr. and Mrs. Snell welcomed me in a gruff kind of way. They warmed up when they learned that Brother and I weren't "rent-hoppers" like some who had "brought down the neighborhood" in the past. The Snells turned out to be good neighbors. When my car wouldn't start one cold morning, Mr. Snell appeared out of nowhere and solved the problem with his jumper cables.

Next door to the Snell's was a rental that housed several earnest and very annoying Jehovah's witnesses. Behind those two houses was a trailer park. In time, I trained my eyes not to see it. To the right of us were the charred remains of a duplex we were told had looked just like ours. Eerie. The gutted house sheltered a homeless person on occasion and was always a hangout for yowling stray cats. We weren't especially enthusiastic about the cats, but they kept the rat population down. Since the burned-out house was owned by Suzanne's realtor boss and current man-friend, she was in a position to promise that the house would be razed and rebuilt soon, very soon. After more than a year, construction began. By then Suzanne had become disenchanted with real estate and her broker man. I think our duplex turned out be the only notch in her sales belt.

To our left, facing the house, was a partially renovated banana-colored duplex, same as ours, minus the upstairs porch. Later, a likable young couple associated with the University moved in, and we became friends. At the end of the little cul-de-sac was yet another duplex, rundown and occupied by students prone to partying hard on weekends. Down the road running parallel to the mill was a granite quarry. Gravel-filled trucks rumbled by at irregular intervals, leaving a trail of rocks and a patina of dust on cars, porches, and any cats that happened to be around. I couldn't allow myself to think about the air quality. It would have spoiled my 'Manhattan apartment by the sea' fantasy.

In summer, I could stand at the back door and pick low-hanging figs for breakfast. If I'd wanted, I could have stood in the same spot, thrown a rock, and probably hit the railroad track. Passing trains caused objects in the apartment to shake and rattle. By the time my three years there ended, I actually missed those howling trains, feeling their vibrations rumbling all through the night. I suppose they were a symbol of my connection to a larger world, a regular reminder that there was life outside my little orbit.

When I told my friend Rodney it was okay to park on the grassy area in the center of the cul-de-sac, he informed me in his best Butch voice,

"Honey, in this neighborhood that's not a cul-de-sac. It's just a dead end."

Rodney helped me fix up the place. By the time we were done, you might think you'd actually walked into a Manhattan apartment. I half expected to see Central Park instead of the trailer park from the living room windows. Not that it was richly furnished, far from it. But that's when I began to develop my own sense of style, finding interesting things that fit my budget. I still have some of those great finds from yard sales, flea markets, and thrift stores. Once I stopped caring what anybody else thought I should like, magic happened. I learned I had hidden talents, a good eye for composition and a passion for color and texture.

The exterior of our duplex was covered with medium-gray siding, possibly chosen to blend with the quarry dust. There was a covered porch with black mailboxes next to the front doors. Brother lived on the right side, as you faced the duplex, next to the burned-out house, I was on the left. Brother kept his shades drawn at all times, and he had a low bar as far as aesthetics went. So, there was no need to draw straws or flip a coin for the left side. My own aesthetics bar was getting higher all the time. I learned that I didn't need fine or fancy, but I did want surroundings that pleased my eye and gave me comfort. In that duplex apartment, I somehow felt free to make that happen for the very first time.

The place was ninety-something years old, with beautifully refinished pine floors. Tall windows still had their original wavy glass panes, and there were three in the spacious living room. Adding to the charm were high ceilings, bead-board in the kitchen, and almost-working fireplaces; they could handle a single synthetic log without great risk. It was what you'd call a "shotgun house." If you shot a gun from the front door and aimed straight, your bullet would go out the back door. The kitchen was behind the living room, with one wall of cabinets, a sink and a stove. Rodney convinced me to move the refrigerator from the far wall into a small space between the kitchen and back door. "The refrigerator cannot be the first thing you see when you walk in." He was right. It was so much nicer his way. That space was intended for a washer and dryer, but it would be worth all the trips to the laundromat to have the fridge out of sight.

Aesthetics had just begun to trump convenience for me, and it still does. With the refrigerator out of the kitchen, there was room for a small pub table and chairs. I found two unfinished rockers on sale, and an old tea crate to use as a table between them along the wall opposite the kitchen cabinets. Just off the "refrigerator space," to the right, was a basic bathroom with shiny new fixtures including a tub-shower. The stairway to a heavenly bedroom was in the kitchen behind the rocking chairs, and there was a closet for the water heater under the stairs. A tall window at the foot of the stairs framed a perfect maple tree, and there was another window at the landing. At the top of the stairs was a built-in desk, actually a slab of Formica with leg room, where I had a receptacle installed for my typewriter. Behind that work area was my closet. The bedroom was large as the living room, with two windows and a single French door. One window held an a/c unit, as did a window in the living room.

Beyond the French door was my favorite feature, a railed porch that ran the length of the house. A gigantic dogwood close to the porch extended its branches in all directions, offering a priceless gift of privacy. I loved that tree. Two folding chairs on my side of the porch, along with a couple of TV trays, made it perfect. I'd pretend to be at the beach as I sat there on many soft nights, even sweltering nights. When it was cold, I'd wrap myself in a blanket. Combining star-gazing with a beer, I decided the whirring looms sounded like the ocean. It was the ocean to me, though that romantic notion probably would have met with contempt from the shift workers laboring inside.

The dogwood wasn't the only contributor to my precious privacy. Brother had no interest in the out-of-doors when he could have air conditioning or heat inside. He often slept on his downstairs couch and rarely came up and out for a visit. So the porch became mine. Sometimes we'd visit back and forth, but we always called or used our knock-on-the-wall code to make sure it was okay. Boundaries were honored even before I knew there was such a thing as boundaries. I doubt Brother has heard of boundaries to this day.

Here's a poem I wrote during my duplex days across from the textile mill:

The Wino

He passes, not seeing me
on the porch, taking what sunshine

is left this autumn afternoon.
Ruddy face, hollow eyes, shoulders
stooped under a sweater thin & worn
as he from too many Novembers.
Is there a coat for winter?
Slow, measured steps, right foot, left,
rounding the corner as two bikers
& a barking hound pass by.

Does the man carry mean memories,
I wonder,
or call up better days for company?

I walk down the block, standing
a long time, watching sunlight
tease the crimson leaves.
I listen to the looms
 whirring inside the cotton mill,
shiver for no reason.
Crackling leaves, feet moving faster
on the return trip, brown paper sack
held close like a life raft.
We exchange nods, I smile.
I look in his eyes and see
 a light has switched on.

We have no words. He moves along,
his mission accomplished,
while I go in search
of other mirrors.

***

When my temp-agency contract was satisfied, I found some freelance work on my own, transcribing hearings for a state agency. A friend who worked there recommended me. I did the transcription without attending the hearings; they already had taken place when I got the assignment. I listened to the cassette tapes on a machine that was far from state-of-the art. Some of the testimony was barely audible. Determining which voices belonged to which participants caused me to rewind the tapes again and again as I struggled to decipher every word.

It was tedious, but I pressed on and soon turned in my first transcript. They were pleased with the work, and I transcribed several more hearings. Even though the work was monotonous, and the pay nothing to write home about, I was relieved to be generating some income.

Sidebar: All the transcription work was done on my portable Smith-Corona, and there was no such thing as auto erase or delete. Each error had to be meticulously corrected. I don't recall whether correction tape or the white correction fluids were on the market then; maybe I still used an eraser. Either way, you can guess how much I treasure the word processing tricks my trusty MacBook can do. And I don't even know half of them.

Neal had spent most of the summer with me, with some time at the duplex and time at his grandparents' playing with his cousins and friends. We saw some movies, swam in my aunt's pool, and had fun on sizzling tennis courts at a city park. We had some special times together. It was excruciating to put him on the plane back to Texas in mid-August. For about a week after he left, I kept forgetting to breathe.

***

I had transcribed all the hearings and gotten a similar job with another agency. By then it was late fall, and I was getting my resume together. I wanted to find a permanent job with benefits and work I would actually enjoy. (At least by the late 70's women were "allowed" to have credit cards. After the divorce in 1973 I had been able to establish credit only because a friend's family owned a local department store, and he personally set up an account in my name.)

When I called a colleague of my father's to ask him to serve as a reference, he offered me a job working for him in the State Senate. He said the offer was contingent on his becoming chairman of the Ethics Committee when the Legislature convened in January. It was an awkward situation. I wasn't comfortable about working in the Senate, although politics and policy always had been in my blood. When I was in school at USC, girls weren't allowed to serve as pages, so I had missed out on that experience. I felt conflicted about Senator Frampton's offer.

Papa had served in the Senate for years and was high in seniority at the time. I told Senator Frampton that my working there might cause criticism, for my father, for him, and for me. He would hear none of that, pointing out that my father didn't serve on the Ethics Committee, so I wouldn't be working for him. I'd rarely even see him at the Capitol. Senator Frampton knew I'd be perfect for the job. Could I wait until January? I don't think I ever said "yes." It was just that the Senator didn't take "no" for an answer.

I knew that, regardless of how good I was at the job, no matter how hard I worked, some people would assume I wasn't earning my keep, that I was hired because of my father. This caused me considerable anxiety. But the Senator blew off my concern, as did my father and the Senate Clerk. "Come to the office before noon on January 12, and you can listen to the intercom and hear when committees are chosen. If I get to be chairman, you got a job. If not, I'll be a reference."

I was saying, "But—" when he wished the family and me a Merry Christmas, and then, "See you on the 12th." Once again, I felt as though my future, even my present, was not in my control. My life, which now included Senator Frampton, was like a tidal wave crashing over me. I could go with the current or drown fighting it. I wasn't sure whether to be grateful or resentful. I chose grateful and kept up the freelance work until the first day of Christmas holidays. That day I felt like a woman out of jail. I was a free spirit, singing my way to the airport to meet my precious son.

***

During that time, except for a couple of "friend fix-ups," I didn't date. One fix-up was with a successful real estate developer who shamelessly promoted himself every minute. He didn't try to hide the fact that he was appalled, and obviously frightened, by my neighborhood where I felt totally comfortable. He left his Mercedes running, locked of course, when he came to the door. I had planned to invite him in for a glass of wine or something. I've never suffered snobs gladly; however, that night I managed to be on good behavior for the sake of the friends who introduced us. On the few occasions I did date, by the end of the first hour I usually wished I were home in my PJ's with a good book or visiting with a friend.

During my three years in the mill village duplex, I was mostly in survival mode, dealing with the absence of Neal in my life and working very hard. I relied on friends for relief from the day-to-day stress. They helped me through those first years back in South Carolina. Actually, friends always have sustained me. Friendship is sacred to me. Most of my social life centered around trusted friends then, as it does today. We made each other laugh. We were comfortable with one another's tears, and we enjoyed soulful, serious, and outrageous conversations. My budget was lean, so I didn't go out often, except for some pleasant evenings among friends at the American Legion watering hole.

Three of my friends were men, editors at the daily newspapers in Columbia. There were morning and afternoon papers at that time. I could count on my pals showing up at the Legion any week night, and occasionally they stopped by on weekends. On Fridays, when I could get out of the office for lunch, I would meet them at a downtown restaurant. These fellows were a little closer to my parents' age than mine, but that never mattered. They were bright, clever, in-the-know, and always good for stimulating conversation and a laugh. I enjoyed matching wits with them, and they liked my sense of humor. They respected the fact that I would not discuss Senate matters, even though there were a few times they'd have liked me to do that. I didn't allow them to get too big for their britches and discouraged them from becoming hopeless cynics.

Among friends who were regulars at "our" bar at the time were a University professor and his wife, other news reporters, and my friend Suzanne. We were two of the very few single woman who spent time there. Several other congenial acquaintances joined us periodically. One editor friend had a "Top Ten Bores List," and some of the guys on it would elbow their way into our circle from time to time. If one of their tales was spectacularly boring, we'd move the teller to the top of The List.

Everybody smoked then, including me. I know, I know. I'm about to cough just thinking about it. When I took up the habit in my teens, we were told cigarettes were good for us, they would calm our nerves. I swear. I no longer smoke and haven't for a long time. In fact, I'm terribly allergic now.

Often, after a couple of drinks, the most dignified editor-friend could be talked into hamming it up with his George M. Cohan medley, and we'd all join in the second time around.

The best thing about it was that nobody "on the outside" would have believed him capable of such frivolity. He had a stern look and manner of speaking that could frighten young children and reporters of any age.

In 1979 and the early 1980's, it was still rare for women to go into bars alone, at least in my provincial city. I was comfortable at the Legion where "everybody knew my name" and knew that my sole interest was being with friends there. I always nursed one beer before switching to ginger ale. Never would drink and drive, although some patrons would take a "toter" for the road when they headed home. Not illegal then.

Sidebar: I have lived in times when a woman was considered far less significant than a man, treated disrespectfully in more overt ways than we sometimes are even today. Objectified. Like racism, it's more subtle now, but both biases remain a sad reality.

One scare tactic intended to derail the Equal Rights Amendment was that we would have to share public restrooms with men if it were passed. That was calculated to silence all but the most dedicated feminists; however, the restroom in the Legion bar was already unisex, so it put the brakes on that foolish talk there. I wish I could tell you I was active in the Women's Movement. I wasn't, although I did write a few pro-ERA letters and usually spoke my mind when the subject came up. Gloria Steinham will always have my respect and admiration. When I'm feeling regretful about my lack of activism, I try to believe this: Maybe I modeled independent living for a few other women at the time. Then again, that's probably wishful thinking.

We owe a huge debt to the women who were active. They put up with a lot and gave up a lot to pave the way to greater equality for us all. They make me think of the "iron jawed angels" who sacrificed so much during the fight for women's suffrage. In fact, the *Iron-Jawed Angels* documentary is well worth seeing if you haven't.

***

Senate jobs often were seen as exciting, even glamorous; neither term described my reality there. When people would go on and on about how exciting my job must be, I'd turn my tongue into a colander rather than scream. When asked where I work, I learned to say, "For the State" or "I'm a government bureaucrat." The questioner usually would stifle a yawn and change the subject.

Nothing about the job was glamorous to me, probably because I grew up with parents who believed no one person is more important than another, regardless of title or celebrity. I always have felt everyone is equally worthy of respect, regardless of wealth, social status, or political power. Most of the people around me didn't share that feeling.

Understand, I admire creative people who work to get better and better at whatever they create. I admire anyone who fights for a worthy cause, and I revere any human who lives with great courage. I find nothing to admire about self-important snobs.

I remember walking back to the State House one night after a reception, thinking about taking my shoes off as soon as I could get to my car. A charming Republican senator, a little older than my father, walked along with me. I liked him even though we were polar opposite in our politics, and he was a glorifier of the Confederacy. The Confederate flag was flying on the State House dome then. (It was several years later that the flag became a major issue and made national news.) The senator pointed to the flag and asked in his exaggerated Southern drawl, "Miss Lucinda, what do you think when you see that noble flag flying up there?" Without skipping a beat, I said, "I think they should take it down." Obviously stunned, he paused a split second, then roared with laughter. "You don't mean that!" When I assured him I was very serious, he teased, "You could end up being the last white Democrat in South Carolina." Fine by me.

My time at the Senate helped hone my authenticity, helped me learn to speak my truth, even to the powerful. I had respect for the Senate as a body and treated members with appropriate decorum at the State House. But after hours, although still respectful, I would speak up more easily than some because power didn't impress or intimidate me.

I can tell you I never experienced my job as exciting in a good way. The salary was inadequate for the level of responsibility and the work load. But it was a job with benefits and I was good at it. Dealing with an FBI sting, testifying in Federal Court, probably having the office phones tapped and, some speculated, maybe even my home phone? Not exciting.

The FBI sting, called "Operation Lost Trust," didn't target me. I simply was responsible for the records of the Senate Ethics Committee, the Economic Interests and Campaign Disclosure reports, and I facilitated those filings. Apparently the sting had been set up to catch lawmakers suspected of taking money in exchange for their votes. As I recall, a major aspect of the case was based on whether the money offered and received was considered a campaign contribution and therefore properly reported. I'm fairly certain that was the case.

One day two undercover agents came to the Committee office saying they were with a public relations firm in Virginia, and I believed them. Fundraisers often came in to comb the files for potential donors. In hindsight, I'm surprised I didn't guess they were agents. They asked more questions than anyone ever had, anyone other than a couple of relentless reporters. And they were wearing the fairly typical "uniform" of blue blazers, gray trousers and oxford shirts. Clean-cut fellows, very buttoned-down.

I gave them access to the records, as I would have done for anyone asking to see them. I understood later that they were checking me out, wanted to be sure I had been operating by the book.

Fortunately, I'm big on ethics myself and always have been a rule follower. I had a reputation for being equally fair to incumbent Senators and candidates alike, regardless of political affiliation. I was helpful, but I wouldn't have allowed anything illegal or unethical to take place in order to "help" anyone, no matter who it might be. And I was careful about record keeping, so I had all the documentation needed to support Committee actions as well as my own.

By the time the Sting happened, there was a new Ethics chairman. When my first chairman lost his Senate race, the Senate Clerk drove over to the home office of the incoming chairman to convince him I should stay on, told him he would never need to worry about the Committee if I continued as administrator. The new chairman had planned to hire someone from his own district, but he decided in favor of my staying on. He told me we would "try it for a while and see how it worked out." Over the years I'd ask him, "Do you think this might work out?" He was a good man, and I was fond of him. I liked that he had a sense of humor and could take a joke. He was even more neurotic than I was, so I felt comfortable working with him. I don't think he ever regretted his decision.

Even knowing I had done everything "by the book," the Sting still was a nerve-shattering experience. The press camped out in the office for weeks, and reporters were calling me at home. My already heavy work load increased beyond belief. I was short on sleep for what seemed like a very long time. I had to copy and personally certify every page of a large number of documents. I'll always be grateful for the help of a conscientious page, a young woman who helped with the photocopying and gave me moral support.

I made arrangements with a Senate Security officer to avoid media coverage of my delivering the documents to the FBI office. I liked the idea of taking them rather than having the Feds coming to get them and perhaps giving the impression they had "seized" the records. I wanted the Committee's cooperation to be very clear. We pulled it off without being followed, and can you imagine this? After all the hoopla of getting every page certified and being so careful to include everything they wanted, I had to ask for a receipt for the boxes of documents! The agent seemed surprised. I felt like a Godfather character when I said, "It's just good business practice." I wasn't going back to the office without a receipt, and I did get one. Only then did the press learn that the FBI had received everything they had requested. They had not needed a subpoena.

Once the investigation was out in the open, the story became national news. "The Sting" is infamous in South Carolina. It was a hard time for me for many reasons: the extra work, being interviewed by attorneys, and the dread of testifying in Federal Court and wondering what day I'd be called, or even what week. The upcoming court appearance was a sword hanging over my head, and I felt absolutely alone in handling it all. My chairman's only comment when I asked for his advice was, "You'll be fine." I'm not an attorney; he was. And I wasn't fine.

I asked a buddy of mine, a respected chief counsel for one of the big committees, to tell me something I might need to know. He said, "I'm just glad it's you and not me."

The criminal proceedings hurt a lot of people, the guilty and the innocent. It was a difficult thing to go through personally and difficult to witness the pain it caused others. I aged a few years in those months.

***

I often went into the office on weekends—not only during the Sting—to keep from sinking in the quicksand of Session days. Those days involved frantic activity surrounding the Senator and his schedule.

With visiting constituents, the pages and the lobbyists, there was little time to take care of the administrative work. No matter how well organized I was, it all went to hell the minute the Senator crossed the threshold. I resigned myself to being a gracious hostess on those days and made sure no one saw me sweat or heard me swear.

After a time, my Ethics Committee chairman moved to a different committee and asked me to go with him. The larger committee had more employees, and he retained that experienced staff, so my work load lightened considerably. I focused mostly on the senator's constituent services and pages, special projects, managing his schedule, and making sure the office ran smoothly.

I began to have some free time, and even some energy, in the evenings and on weekends. I began taking accumulated vacation days here and there on non-Session days. I had developed a burning interest in health and integrative medicine, so I started a small nonprofit organization to advance the cause. I went through the incorporation process and applied to the IRS for 501 (c)(3) status without an attorney or accountant. I did show the application to an attorney friend who thought the document looked okay. I recruited a board of directors and other volunteers. I look back and wonder how I was able to do what I did, working at home on weekends and late on week nights for the nonprofit. I was painfully conscientious about not allowing the nonprofit work to overlap with the Senate job; I drew a clear line between my paying job and the health advocacy organization. I made my nonprofit phone calls and contacts either in the evenings or at lunchtime. For special events or circumstances, I sometimes was able to take accrued annual leave. Immersion in the service of advancing that cause became my "hobby" for eight years.

We provided programs and services to the community on a small scale, smaller than I wish had been the case. But I've been reminded that it wasn't small to the people we served, and we did raise awareness about the importance of a whole-person approach to health and healing. Had we all not needed our paying jobs, been able to devote "prime time" to it, the organization might have grown into something much larger. I wish ... well, I wish it had grown into a match for my vision of what it could have been. But *if wishes were horses ....*

It had seemed important to advocate for a return to more compassionate, humanistic care in a time when sophisticated medical tests and prescription drugs were distancing doctors more and more from the humanity of practice. And I was determined to do that in a positive way. One program I conceived, and with the help of generous volunteers made a reality, was the Physician of the Year Award for exceptional compassion in the practice medicine. That award continued to grow in scope and stature each year. My friend Jan, who took on the project after the first few years, turned it into an impressive uptown event. It became a big deal in the Capital City and the Midlands medical community. When I went as a guest to the last "Top Doc" gala, I was astonished by how much that program had grown and what an elegant evening it was. I felt good about what we had done in the early days and absolutely was bursting with pride about where Jan had taken "Top Doc" since I had moved away and left the organization in her capable hands. She deserved far more accolades that night than I did. Nevertheless, I received both praise and an armful of beautiful flowers to take home. The greatest gift of the night was the sense of closure I felt as I walked off stage. It was past time for my "baby" to be fully committed to the care of others.

My Senate experiences could fill another book. Probably I should I wait until everybody's dead before writing it; problem is, "everybody" would include me!

***

After spending nearly three school years with his father, Neal came to live with me in Columbia. The previous semester he and Ben had moved from Texas to the South Carolina town where Ben grew up. Neal was utterly miserable there.

After Neal came to Columbia, Ben moved back to Texas and married a lovely woman I would come to like and respect. I found a house that would place Neal in a school district with an excellent drama teacher. In fact, it was there Neal gave a riveting performance as a young man suffering with mental illness. Broadway quality, I say, even if I am his mother.

Neal's teenage years were challenging for both of us. Our love didn't go away, but it went into hiding on occasion. Ultimately, Neal decided to go Texas for his senior year and live with Ben and his wife. Hard as some of the hard times had been, I hated to see him go. I experienced a lot of grief around his decision and a sense of having failed at parenting my teenage son. Today I know I did a fairly good job under some difficult circumstances.

Neal ping-ponged back to me after he finished school and was looking for work. Despite strongly encouraging him to go to college, he was stronger in his resolve not to go. Ultimately, that proved to be a good decision. He found temporary or part-time radio jobs in Columbia before settling into a long-term broadcasting career in the Northeast.

He has experienced a lot of healing and growth since then and made a good life for himself. I have believed that setting Neal free to live his adult life, without the emotional albatross of a needy or hovering single mother, has been the greatest gift I could give him. We are in touch regularly and visit when we can. I deeply love and respect the man Neal has become. He and his wife Lee are fine parents, and their daughter is a secure, dearly-loved child. I call her my "Bliss Bringer."

In fact, when other grandparents talk about things they "wish" their kids would or wouldn't do in bringing up the grandchildren, I'm at a rare loss for words. I can check out of those conversations and mentally count my blessings or make a grocery list. I'm glad Lee and Neal both lived through earlier marriages that didn't work out and experienced significant personal growth before marrying and bringing a child into the world. There's a lot to be said for mature parenting.

***

I'm thinking about a time when Neal was visiting at the Mill duplex. Since I had only one bedroom, he slept on a cot. I was about to wake him one morning when I noticed his big, almost-man feet hanging over the end of the cot. It was a poignant moment, the joy of having him there with me mixed with sadness that he was growing up so fast. And, knowing that times like this, just the two of us together, would be rare before long, as he matured and began his independent life. I stood watching him sleep, wishing his younger years could have been "normal" whatever that looks like. But *if wishes were horses ....*

Later that day Neal and I took a "memory ride" at his request. It included driving by our first house, the apartment by the park where he played Little League and injured his hand the day I didn't come straight home from work because I knew he would be at practice. We drove by his school and kindergarten, the neighborhood store where he remembered walking with a buddy for the first time instead of with his mama. I remembered pacing until he was safely home. We stopped for a few minutes at another shadier park where I would take him as a toddler and pre-schooler. On hot summer days he'd splash in the wading pool, and I could still see myself responding to his plea to push him *higher, nooo, higher* in the swing.

After our tour, I told him I'd been thinking about his childhood, knew it hadn't been as easy or as good as it should have been. He gave me a puzzled look, as if I were speaking Mandarin. Then, with unmistakable sincerity, he said that his childhood had been great, all of it. Sometimes things aren't as we have believed them to be, after all; sometimes that can be a relief.

Neal continues to occupy the VIP suite in my heart, now sharing it with Lee and their daughter E.G. The relationship between Neal and me hasn't always been easy, but it is always real, deep and glorious. Being his mother has allowed me to love as I never dreamed I could love. Even when I was struggling to love myself.

***

Before closing this segment of *Dancing on Mars,* there's something I want to square with myself and share with you: I've often said my life has been nearly risk-free, that I've been inclined to play it safe. That I've been inclined that way is true. It is also true that I have taken some significant risks. And it's good to be able to see that now.

In my family of origin some unhealthy patterns have been passed on from generation to generation. That can happen in families unless and until someone intentionally breaks a pattern or cycle. I can see now that I have been able to say "no more" to some of the unhealthier familial ways of being. There's no doubt I still carry some of the family patterns. But waking up to their existence and examining them has been the beginning of some significant cycle-breaking.

Our family, in general, has a penchant for denying situations that are unpleasant or beg confrontation, especially anything involving strong feelings like anger or grief. Although confrontation remains uncomfortable for me even now, I no longer keep silent in the face of such things as meanness, religious and racial intolerance, or other injustices I witness. I remind myself that it's okay to say what I mean and mean what I say, as long as I don't say it mean.

When I hear someone talk about "the elephant in the living room"—ignoring a situation that appears too big not to be obvious—I sometimes say, "There was a whole *herd* of elephants in our living room." Most family members have a hard time relating to someone who doesn't deal in denial or pretty half-truths. To live my own life authentically, I risked feeling like the outsider, having a sense of not belonging in our family. And indeed I often have felt that way. Ironic that, although I'm the "foreigner," I've been most involved in the trials and tribulations that come with the family package. Partly because of being the oldest and, more significantly, because of my hyper-vigilant sense of responsibility.

At the moment I'm thinking of risks taken even before therapy, before making any conscious efforts toward personal growth. As a child, I would offer up my love to Emma and Mammy; I risked rejection by allowing them to see my strong emotions and physical evidence of my love for them. Mammy always was a little twitchy about that, and Emma might or might not temporarily reject me at any given time. Even when disapproval was strong, I usually felt their love; however I felt their love had to be earned, and I often felt shamefully unworthy.

To question the church's teachings throughout my life has been, and continues to be, a huge risk in the context of family and every relevant segment of society in the South's "Bible Belt" where I choose to live. It was especially frightening to risk my mother's approval, acceptance, and, for all I knew as a child, her love. As an adult, my beliefs are incompatible with most of my relatives' beliefs, and sometimes I feel judged for that. And I judge them sometimes, too, even though I respect their right to believe as they do.

These days most of my friends enjoy, as I do, living non-religious, deeply spiritual lives. Those few friends affiliated with mainstream religious traditions not only are respectful of my spirituality, but also supportive. Still, I have risked losing the acceptance of neighbors, colleagues, potential mates, and even a tennis partner once, because I don't belong to a church. I will talk more about that next in Hundreds of Ways to Kneel.

Living out loud has been an ongoing risk, not only with family but with some I considered close friends. Sometimes my "friendship closet" has been cleaned when I have spoken honestly or stood up for myself.

Losing certain longtime friends has been painful. Only with the passage of time have I understood that "losing" those relationships was for my highest good all along. The losses were a necessary part of my growth.

The family pattern of keeping secrets and burying unpleasant emotions is cracked, although not completely broken. With the support of therapist Jack, I gradually began to risk expressing feelings that I needed to make clear, even when it meant making myself vulnerable to the judgment or power others. This seemed radical in the beginning, until I became unwilling to experience dis-ease as a result of stuffing my feelings any longer, simply so others wouldn't feel uncomfortable. Neal understands the importance of feeling his feelings. I have encouraged him in that his whole life, even before I was able to express many of my own. I trust he never had anyone say to him, "You know you don't feel that way." My feelings were often "corrected" by the adults in my life, edited even more often than my manners.

Taking steps to change family patterns takes the willingness of only one individual; it doesn't involve recruiting other family members. I say that not to make myself out to be a martyr or a saint. I tried martyrdom for years and managed to recover, and sainthood wouldn't be much of a kick even if I qualified.

Reflecting on my life so far, an old saying comes to mind: *If all our troubles were hanging on a line, you'd choose yours, and I'd choose mine.* I believe there's something to that. I also believe Life is sweeter than any troubles it sends our way. Don't you?

***

Sweet

Yes, I know
there is war
and hunger,
the Earth
and her
children
weeping.

Still, life is sweet,

sun waking me with
soft caresses, a crow
announcing his place
in the scheme of things,
morning coffee rich
with chocolate and cream.

A shower-stage for my opera,
to wash myself clean as this
new day. Body hosting tap-water
rivers streaming over mountains,
splashing a geography of
mossy-floored forest, mountains
and valley humming with
earth body's warm secrets,
 rising
          falling
                    with the breath
of each moment's new surprise.

Who in truth is wise enough
to pronounce one thing

a blessing,
another a curse?
Stand up if you are such a wise one.

Me, I know that I do not know,
that I simply am here, awake
in the experience, and
Life is sweet.

Part II

Hundreds of Ways to Kneel - Reflections on a Spiritual Journey

Today, like every other day, we wake up empty
and frightened. Don't open the door to the study
and begin reading. Take down a musical instrument.

Let the beauty we love be what we do.
There are hundreds of ways to kneel and kiss the ground.

~from *The Essential Rumi* translated by Coleman Barks

It took a long time finding my own way to "kneel and kiss the ground."

In my little segregated South Carolina town, there was no such thing as religious diversity. White folks were Baptists, Episcopalians, Methodists and Presbyterians—in our case Associate Reformed Presbyterians. The town was in a collective state of shock when a family of Catholics moved in. They couldn't have been more exotic if they'd arrived in a spaceship. They drove more than thirty miles to Columbia for Mass. Was it true, we wondered, that they ate only fish and did everything the Pope ordered them to do? There was only one Jew, our optometrist, but he lived in Columbia and commuted to his office on Main Street.

Growing up I went, with and without various combinations of family, to Sunday School and morning services at the ARP Church. I've been told the Associate Reformed Presbyterians came into being after a split with Presbyterians over whether to sing psalms or hymns. Big fight. The more conservative ARP's insisted on sticking with psalms. Most of the psalms, put to music, seemed heavy to me, sad. Even our impressive choir and superior organist couldn't lift me up with "By the rivers of Babylon where we sat down, we wept, yea we wept, as we remembered Zion." For some reason that was Papa's favorite.

One of few early childhood memories is bedtime at my grandmother Mammy's house. "Let's say our prayers," she'd say, kneeling by her side of the bed. I would kneel on my side. The silence before her Amen lasted forever. I had no idea she was thinking prayers in her head. I thought kneeling silently for a long time was prayer. Maybe I was an early meditator.

For our family, going to church was more about pleasing my grandmother than communing with the Almighty. From the family pew, I heard that God was a jealous God. There was talk about sin and Hell. If you didn't believe in Jesus Christ as the son of God who died for your sins, you could count on going to Hell. He was your Savior, and you'd better believe it. Not a comforting message for a child, or adult for that matter. Even worse for me, and more confusing, was learning that this all-powerful, all-knowing God the Father loved the world so much that he allowed his son Jesus to be nailed to a cross and brutally murdered. What kind of sense did that make? What a mean father Jesus had! Whatever happened to God is great and God is good? I couldn't accept all the Christian contradictions, even as a child. As an adult, I'm about as far from being Fundamentalist as a person can get. I don't take the Biblical texts literally, no matter who's spinning what part of it. I have more than a little concern about the theocrats who seem to have big plans for us all.

Growing up I witnessed hypocrisy aplenty. Judgment was in the minister's spotlight more than love ever was, along with an abundance of mixed messages. God and Jesus loved all people the same, but anybody who didn't believe exactly like He wanted them to believe would be condemned to Hell. God is Love, yet I was shaken as a child to hear a deacon say that if a Negro walked into our church—God's house, not the deacon's—he would walk out. I was perplexed and appalled by the insanity of that. Even at age ten I knew the deacon's statement had nothing to do with the kind of love I wanted to feel for my Creator and other humans.

I was baptized, or christened, as an infant and became a member of the church when I was about twelve. I could name all the books of the Bible and recite the Catechism. My church-joining didn't involve much in the way of Divine inspiration. It simply was what my peers were doing at the time, and it was expected. Plus, sometimes there were coke floats after the classes.

By the time I was thirteen, I was teaching a Sunday school class of four and five-year-olds. Around that time I also convinced my mother to let me wear high heels to church and put my hair up in a bun. Playing the role of an adult, I guess I thought I should look like one. No doubt, what I looked like was a fool.

I have memory images of children sitting around a long, low table coloring or drawing, and one little boy who was a handful. I read children's Bible stories to them. I didn't take my doubts into the Sunday school classroom. I stayed in character wherever I went, the overly responsible "good girl" everyone wanted.

I did veer from my people-pleasing, good-girl behavior in one respect during my early teens. I began challenging my mother on specific beliefs and conflicting Biblical teachings. She had no answers. Undoubtedly, her sincere objective was to get me into Heaven. She thought I needed to have more faith and ask fewer questions. I should "trust God." She thought this God was trustworthy? "You just think too much," she'd say when exasperated with my questions.

Some Sunday mornings I'd beg off going to church. Mama would be in bed, having her breakfast on a tray. She'd call out for me to hurry and get ready for church; we wouldn't want Mammy to be the only one in our pew. Whatever would people think? Mammy, petite Victorian matriarch that she was, held great power over my parents. They'd even hide their drinks if her car pulled into the driveway during their happy hours. It was comedic in a way, but I thought it dishonest, too. When I asked Mama why they hid the booze, she said that Mammy didn't approve of drinking. Which didn't answer my question. What was the benefit of being an adult if you couldn't do whatever you wanted in your own house?

I don't mean to paint my grandmother as a humorless Victorian. She actually had a sense of humor and could tell a great story. I'm remembering how she could mimic a person perfectly and have listeners in stitches. And I was able to "soften her up" a little over the years. She was a kind, stoic woman who weathered hard times, even tragedy, with tremendous grace and dignity.

Sunday mornings I was recruited to see that this or that reluctant sibling got dressed in time for Sunday school. Mama went to church sometimes, and sometimes both she and my father would go. But mostly he headed to his office Sunday mornings after making us pancakes. Mama read a devotional every morning at breakfast, ignoring my eye-rolling and the assorted bickering at the table. It wasn't going to be her fault if her children didn't get through the Pearly Gates.

When my mother went to church, I usually could talk her into letting me stay home to clean the house. Emma didn't work Sundays, so it suited Mama to come home to a magazine-cover clean kitchen. All the

Saturday-night ashtrays were washed and the beds were made. I made sure to do an excellent job in exchange for that precious Sunday morning freedom.

Even though I couldn't buy what the Church was selling, I was seriously anxious, at times, about the possibility of Hell. Suppose there really was something to that? My intellect said, "Of course there's not," and anxiety taunted, "But are you *sure*?" Much fear and resentment were percolating, but I couldn't identify those feelings then. Over time, the fears diminished and the resentments grew. At some point I was delighted to learn the word Agnostic, and began to think of myself as one of those rather than an Atheist. I wasn't sure I didn't believe in God. I just rejected the one everybody in my corner of the world was worshipping.

In my teens, I still went to church fairly often, but I wouldn't take communion. That was my bottom line. And I wouldn't repeat the litany of words I didn't believe. Apparently I was acquiring some personal ethics and consequently practicing less hypocrisy. I can't remember how I managed to dodge communion without accounting to my grandmother. I probably implied that cramps or a headache compelled me to leave early. I worked with the tools I knew how to use, but I was uncomfortable telling less than the truth.

***

Fast-forwarding to just after Neal was born, I became active in a Presbyterian Church in Columbia, South Carolina, not out of newfound piety, but because I had taken on the traditional idea that Neal should be brought up in a church. If you ask exactly how I arrived at that, I couldn't tell you. Maybe osmosis, maternal guilt in the DNA. Who knows? Ben would go with baby Neal and me occasionally, but not regularly. At one time he worked Sunday afternoons and took Sunday mornings to relax, most often with a round of golf. Neal was christened in the Presbyterian Church with only our families present to witness his full-throated protests.

I accepted church nursery duty for a year. I even attended circle meetings where some members debated, at great length, which service projects were most worthy of undertaking. One night, instead of staying home to watch a much-anticipated Frank Sinatra special, I listened to a tedious discussion on taking cookies to a nursing home versus doing something else; the nursing home was booked with do-gooders for the next few months. Now that I'm a recovering hypocrite, I wouldn't go to one of those meetings on a dare. Certainly I wouldn't have missed another hour of Sinatra. That was before we had the ability to record or delay programs to accommodate our busy lives.

***

Later, in the '80's, I would work with the clinical psychologist I've mentioned. Jack's bottom line was "What are you feeling in your body now?" It took about two years in therapy with this amazing man before I fully understood what that meant. My work with Jack had a significant positive impact on my spiritual growth, and I learned that spirituality is a journey from the head to the heart.

I remember telling Jack something in a session one day, and he responded in his gentle, melodious voice, "What you're saying seems very sad to me. Why are you smiling?" Damned if I knew. Conditioning? Wear the mask, regardless. Don't pause long enough to feel anything. That happened many times before authentic feelings were unearthed and finally became identifiable. More and more, my affect began to mirror whatever feelings I was having. "Getting in touch with my feelings," knowing what they were and fully feeling them, was a long process.

Laughter always had been enthusiastically received at our house. Anger, on the other hand, was not acceptable. Nor were tears, except sometimes in circumstances involving blood. More times than I could possibly count, my feelings were invalidated, discounted, or edited by my mother and grandmother. "You know you don't feel that way," they'd say. Especially when I would let my passion show. Passion, nothing more than the enthusiasm of youthful vitality, made them very uncomfortable. For me, getting in touch with a lifetime of stifled feelings was scary, gut-wrenching, and expensive work, but it helped me reclaim my vitality, my sometimes-ecstatic life force.

Writing this made me think of something I heard for the first time at a workshop; I still agree with what e.e. Cummings said is "the hardest battle a person can fight." That battle is to be yourself when everyone in your life is trying to make you into somebody else. For me, it has been a lifelong battle.

Beneath a mix of pain, fear, and disillusionment there was a yearning for connection. It would take years to recognize that those feelings weren't only about my divorce or relationship to family or childhood trauma. They were about feeling disconnected from my Source. Mine was a spiritual hunger, something like homesickness, but I didn't understand for a long time what I was homesick for.

***

Jack had been the therapist of a friend who was thriving after working with him. She told me, "If you don't have peace in your life, everything else you have is worthless." Even though I began seeing Jack sometime in 1981, it would be a long time before I had anything resembling peace of mind. But connecting with him did give me something early on—hope. I learned, over time, that Jack was highly regarded by his peers in psychotherapy and behavioral medicine. I heard that was true on a national level. He is a thoroughly good and ethical man with sensibilities in sync with mine. He turned out to be exactly who I needed. My spiritual journey is so interwoven with Jack and our work together that it's impossible to separate them.

Even now I'm not sure whether Jack was aligned with a specific spiritual path. My guess is he's probably a Heinz 57 like me and would avoid limiting himself with a label. He once invited me to a meditation class he was teaching at a local church. He didn't push, just said I might find it interesting. I think he knew it would be a big leap for me. It was a leap, and I took it.

I took my anxious self to those meditation classes every Monday evening for six weeks. It got easier each week because both format and instructor were completely non-threatening. There were no questions, tests, or shaming traps involved. Here, for the first time in years, or ever, I was trusting a man emotionally. I knew early on that Jack wouldn't let me down, and he never did.

With meditation, as with nearly every learning experience, I didn't get bogged down in an academic approach; instead I followed Nike's advice, Just *do it.* Sometimes simply diving into a new thing works for me, especially now that I'm not looking for perfection. When something doesn't work, I try to remember that mistakes are excellent teachers. Starting over is allowed.

Jack taught me a lot and helped me heal some of my broken places. During the decade I worked with him, I usually had a session every week or two, sometimes taking sabbaticals until I was willing to dive once again into the wreckage of my Self. There were times in later years when I saw Jack for one or a series of appointments to work on specific issues. He was a true healer, a rock, an authentic and deeply kind human being. Up to that time, I hadn't known many authentic people. I wanted some of what he had: the realness, the quiet confidence tempered with humility, and the peace that emanated from him regardless of circumstances. His ability to be comfortable in his very own skin. He was a role model worthy of respect.

So, with Jack's support beginning in the early 1980's, I delved into some self-help and personal growth books and articles, most of them with at least sprinklings of spirituality. I became willing to embrace the mystery of Being. I decided I didn't need to know all the answers, or even the questions. By then I was no longer concerned about "Hell."

***

There continue to be bumps in the road on my spiritual journey, and I'm sorry to report that none have been speed bumps. I've finally accepted that there is no destination. It's a lifelong process: lots of shedding old ways of thinking and being, and making space for new gifts such as trust and peace and gratitude. There's lots of "one step forward, two or three back." Periods of recognizable progress and periods of—what? Rest, I suppose. And restlessness.

I remember hearing someone verbalize my feeling that I am part of Creation and Creator. What was said gave me affirming chill-bumps: *I think of God as the ocean and all of creation as drops in the ocean.* Another chill-bumps affirmation came with this teaching: *Enlightenment is only a recognition, not a change at all. The light is in you now.*

As I write this today, I understand a higher reason for Neal's staying in Texas with Ben during the school year. I mean, beyond Ben's convincing me it was best for Neal and beyond his vow to fight me if I insisted on having Neal with me in South Carolina. I know now, as I only sensed then, that I was dying there. My spirit was dying a little each day.

Now I can see the breadth of work I needed to do in order to heal spiritually. That healing could not have begun as it did had I been devoting my energy to Neal's well-being on a daily basis, dividing my energy between Neal and earning a living. I know now, as Neal says about experiences in his own life, that it was "a God thing."

***

Some of my life lessons have come through pain, others through love and tremendous joy. I remember saying at one point that I'd heard about a "dark night of the soul," but I didn't know "dark nights" were multiple and ongoing. The good thing about "dark nights" at this point in my life is that the darkness might be the same, but *I'm* not the same. Today I know how to navigate those times. I know how to love myself through them and ride them out.

I'll never forget Bernie Siegel, MD, sharing this thought in a workshop, "The goal of self-healing is not to change yourself into a better person, but to love yourself and express more of who you really are." It was just what I needed to hear at the time. Even now, I sometimes need to be reminded of that.

One of my "dark night" impressions is the sense of swimming against a strong, angry tide. Now I don't struggle to get anywhere or fight those currents. I simply surrender to the situation and float. I relax into it and allow it to take me where it will. I usually remember to get into my "observer self" and watch what's going on with interest and without judgment when I can manage to do that. Best of all, now I know the dark nights will end. They always do.

Just last week I heard someone say, "Religious people worry about going to Hell; spiritual people have been there already." Amen and amen.

***

How did I get from my spiritual starting point to where I am today? How has the little girl kneeling in silence beside her grandmother's bed, the growing girl who couldn't accept the teachings of her church or the jealous God of her ancestors; how did this atheist/agnostic become someone who loves and feels deeply connected to her Creator? How did she come to know she is beloved by God? She who refuses to squeeze that vast love into a formula, doctrine, or belief system? She who rarely speaks of her beliefs because no words can express the depth and wonder of her spirituality?

The spiritual journey, for me, is not about the mind, although learning certainly is involved. As I've said, it truly is a journey from the head to the heart. I have come to understand that religious doctrines, theologies—any that profess "knowing for sure"—can be roadblocks to experiencing spiritual connection by way of the heart. For me, a strictly intellectual approach would spoil the joy of embracing the great mysteries of Being. And that doesn't mean I ignore reason. Not at all.

How did I get where I am today? With a lot of help. And by striving, often failing, to keep my heart and mind open. I see my beliefs as dynamic, mostly sensory, heart-based, and beyond words. Definitely not debatable. Theology can be argued endlessly, but there's no arguing love. My spirituality is too profound and too personal to debate or even discuss. So I don't. I'm not interested in winning anyone over to feeling, thinking or believing as I do. I respect the right of all people to believe and practice whatever spiritual tradition or religion they choose. I honor all love-based spiritual paths, even though I don't practice them all myself.

Since I respect the right of others to believe as they choose, I expect—no, now I insist— on that same respect. I don't suffer proselytizing graciously. Because she thought I needed saving, a zealous fundamentalist once said, "I feel sorry for you." How much arrogance does it take to say that to a person?

Although there is no destination in my ongoing spiritual journey, there have been milestones along the way, periods of personal growth and life changes for the better. For example, so much of my life I felt defensive when asked, "Where do you go to church?" In my native South, that's the norm, not even considered intrusive by most people! My dilemma was this: I wouldn't lie, but the truth, "I don't go to church," opened the door for all sorts of pressure and harmony disruption. I could see a questioner's eyes light up at the prospect of winning another soul for the kingdom.

Sometimes I allowed humor to be my salvation, saying I worship at Sinking Springs, meaning I slept late on Sunday mornings. Sometimes people didn't get it, most likely assuming mine was one of the many small churches peppering the Southern landscape. And, for those who did get it, laughter usually diffused the situation enough for me to change the subject.

For a good while now I've been comfortable saying, without fluffing it up, that I choose not to attend church. If the inquisitor is particularly obnoxious, I might say I'm Buddhist or an "elastic Christian." Both are true. I saw a bumper sticker the other day that said "I'm for separation of church and hate." And my fairy goddaughter gave me one, spelled out in symbols of assorted faiths, that says *Coexist*. The last road-raging guy who flipped me off in traffic had a bumper sticker proclaiming "God is my co-pilot."

I'm not sure I ever made a conscious decision to explore spirituality. I can't pinpoint a date when it all began. As I said, it seems to have evolved as an integral part of the work I did with Jack. From him I learned that there was another way to "be," rather than living at one extreme or the other within the church I knew or being an Atheist. Maybe making my first appointment with Jack was the beginning.

***

After opening myself to spiritual exploration, it was amazing how many books, people, situations and events found their way into my life. You might have heard the old saying, *When the student is ready, the teacher will appear.* My teachers have taken many forms. Sometimes the teacher has been a conversation overheard in a checkout line or a TV documentary I wouldn't have considered interesting enough to watch a year before. Sometimes it's a person or a book. I was wide open to learning about any spiritual tradition that was based on love. I'm a kinesthetic, experiential learner and more visual than auditory. Although not academically inclined, I have done, and still do, a lot of reading.

I didn't hesitate to "sail into the mystic" when drawn to metaphysical concepts. For example, I became interested in reincarnation. In fact, I had two compelling past-life "memories" I didn't go looking for. The first happened in a session with Jack; the second came during the wedding ceremony of my friends Pat and John as I stood up with them in their church. With my back to the congregation, I was facing a huge cross. The ceremony felt intense, seemed endless as I struggled not to pass out. My knees were buckling and perspiration beading on my clammy skin. Thankfully the happy couple didn't realize it. Somehow I managed to regain composure for the celebration afterwards, my wobbly legs returning to almost normal just in time for the dancing.

Jack, and my exploration of reincarnation, inspired this poem:

You

If from a mist over some foreign sea
you spiral your Self into being,
or in a field of daisies dance into life
on the four leaves of a green clover
or come from the bones of a great silver fish
or as a raindrop falling
on a place long rainless,
whether you appear as liquid light
in the weary eyes of an old man
or emerge from a deep river bed,
red clay kissing your fingers,
from a mother's soft belly
or the belly of a huge round ship,
I would know you
though I might not read the text of your face
I would surely know you.

If in centuries beyond this time
you take birth
whatever body, whatever circumstance,
whether in this place or far away,
through a door hidden altogether from me,
I will know you are here or there,
Back
beyond names, beyond language,
beyond the shadows of reason.

I will know
and once again my heart will be glad
you are.

***

At lunchtime one Friday I walked from my office in the State Senate building to the public library downtown. I planned to pick up something to read over the weekend, something light after a trying work week. It was an exceptionally hot day, and I went directly to the cool, dim area at the back, standing between the long rows of shelves to catch my breath. I had no idea what section I was in, only glad no one was there to see me mopping perspiration from my face. As I stood there cooling off, a book fell from a high shelf for no apparent reason. *A Meditator's Diary* by Jane Hamilton-Merritt landed at my feet. I hadn't heard of the book or the author.

As I said, once I opened to the idea of spiritual exploration, the teachers appeared. I'd have been a foolishly stubborn skeptic not to believe this book had fallen at my feet for a reason, and that night I settled in to read it. Hamilton-Merritt, PhD, a Viet Nam war correspondent, wrote about her experiences in Thailand monasteries. The impact of what she shared in the book was profound. I related deeply to her feelings, and I had a "knowing" that everything was okay. That I was okay. I was perfectly safe and acceptable just as I was. I burst into tears of relief and wept for a long time. Whatever triggered that is what I wish I could remember.

Another significant book for me early on was Carl Jung's *Memories, Dreams, and Reflections.* As a boy, Jung enjoyed walking in the woods with his father, an Episcopal minister. He talked about how he felt being in the woods, how connected to his spiritual being. Sadly, I'm unable to quote the part that nearly took my breath away. What I remember was the sense that the farther away he was from a church, the closer he felt to God. Being in Nature was what fed his spirit. In fact, my "Sinking Springs" response was retired once I opted to paraphrase Dr. Jung on why I don't attend church. Nature is my cathedral-of-choice, too.

***

In my early years of "seeking," I attended various churches just to see whether my feelings had changed over time. The Unitarian Fellowship was the closest I came to thinking I could embrace a church. I liked their accepting attitude, apparent lack of dogma, and the positive energy there. But I have learned that any organized form of spirituality, "organized religion," has no appeal for me. Churches, whether the impressive cathedral, a charming country church, the mega church with its celebrity pastor, or the non-denominational strip-mall church that insists it isn't a church, all involve politics, budgets, doctrine, socializing, and inevitable in-fighting, none of which I want in my spiritual life. I won't risk diminishing the precious, private connection I cherish with my Creator whom I usually call God; a God who is part of me.

I want to be clear that, although I don't take the Bible literally, I respect some of its teachings as well as teachings from other texts that are considered sacred. I admire, and strive to follow, the lessons Jesus taught. I'm happy for people who are nourished spiritually at their chosen synagogues, churches, mosques and any other place of worship. The aspect of community, with the sense of belonging and mutual support, holds great appeal for some. And that's a good thing. It's just not good for me. I'm enthusiastic about the idea of every human using the personal freedom we have to search for meaning, wherever that quest may lead, or wherever it doesn't. However you do it, wherever you begin, wherever you go, I believe it's worthwhile. Actually, it's more than worthwhile. Broadening our horizons, expanding consciousness, and awakening our awareness of the present moment—what could be more energizing, more enlivening?

There seems to be an over-abundance of information in our twenty-first century world and far too little wisdom. I see the pursuit of spiritual growth, and a willingness to delve more deeply into life, as worthy goals. May we continue to grow in wisdom and in truth. As I heard a wise woman say, "We don't grow old; we become old from not growing."

***

Once on a plane heading back to Columbia from New York, I noticed a young woman across the aisle reading poetry; at least the text I saw was arranged on the page like poems. After landing, I told her I'd seen that she was reading a book of poems. (It's not often this poetry lover sees people reading poems on planes, or anywhere else for that matter.) She responded warmly, "Oh, no, it's a cosmic book." I had no idea what she meant, but she held up *Emmanuel's Book* by Pat Rodegast. "It's good," she said, smiling. We chatted a few minutes during what otherwise would have been a tedious time on the runway before approaching the gate. We exchanged contact information, and I made a note about the book. By "cosmic" she had meant metaphysical or spiritual.

A couple of months had passed when my brother D told me he'd met someone I had met in New York. I had visited a friend in the City and hadn't met anyone there from South Carolina. I thought he was pulling my leg, as he is apt to do. He couldn't convince me otherwise until he remembered she'd been reading a book that I thought was poetry. Then I realized it was Callie from the plane. She'd been with someone he knew at a restaurant earlier that week. As brother D says, "It's a small world, but I wouldn't want to paint it."

A few days after seeing my brother, I was at my favorite consignment shop when I heard voices on the other side of the skirt rack. One voice sounded familiar. In a few minutes I literally bumped into Callie! She told me about meeting my brother, and we agreed that we were meant to know one another. So, we met for a glass of wine after work the following week. I finally bought a copy of *Emmanuel's Book,* and it remains one of my favorites today, along with *Emmanuel's Books* 2 and 3. Being reminded of Callie and running into her before we finally got together was synchronicity in action. And I learned from that experience to pay attention when it happens. Often synchronistic situations have led to the next step in my spiritual growth.

Callie and I once took a late-autumn road trip with other "seekers" to a Medicine Wheel Gathering in the mountains of Alabama. There we studied with Brook Medicine Eagle, Wallace Black Elk and other respected Native teachers. This took place off-season at a boys' camp where we slept on lumpy bunks in cabins without heat or hot water for showers. I loved every minute of it. There was beautiful ceremonial dancing and drumming. Presenters mingled easily with participants offering rich opportunities for conversation. We were awakened each morning by the sounds of a Native flute calling us to the Medicine Wheel. It was a major experience.

Sidebar: Three times I planned to be part of a Sweat Lodge, and all three times I was unable to participate in this very hot, very powerful Native American prayer ceremony. Why? Because a menstruating woman isn't allowed to enter the Lodge! I was incensed, thinking that, like some other religions, the Native Americans must consider women inferior, unclean, and unacceptable at that time of the month. Actually, I learned that the opposite is true, yet another lesson about judging and jumping to conclusions. In Native American culture women are seen as powerful beings, especially during their menses. The concern is that the strong energy of a menstruating woman might overwhelm the prayer energy in the Lodge. So after three strikes, I concluded I'm not meant to pray in a Sweat Lodge. However, I did serve as doorkeeper once for a Lodge deep in the South Georgia woods. Earnest in my sacred duty I stood silently for three hours in what I would later learn was poison oak or ivy, feeding the mosquitoes.

***

Sometime in 2006 a postcard came from my friend Pat: "Reserve mid-June through the first week of July of next year ... Southwest road trip! We'll go to Chaco Canyon for Solstice sunrise." The postcard showed a glossy photo of the ruins at Chaco. Pat and her husband John had learned about the Solstice celebration when they visited Chaco the previous year and I had been intrigued by Robert Redford's PBS documentary, "The Legend of Chaco Canyon." I always had been drawn to mystical places, and Chaco was such a place.

Just after reading Pat's message, I was excited. Then my neurotic needs for comfort and control took excitement hostage, and I began thinking about how I'd get my needs met on the road. Could I make it on almonds and cereal bars if they wanted fast food? Being strongly attached to my home, I don't often go away for more than three or four days at a time. How would I survive the shift from my solitary existence to the constant company of two other humans, even humans I know well and love dearly? And being in the back seat always has guaranteed motion sickness for me. I also realized that, as much as I value love and connection, I was about to allow fear to sabotage an opportunity to experience both in a big way. What a gift it was to be included in this trip!

Still, I'd get sweaty palms thinking about John and Patsy's high energy and fitness levels. No way I could keep up with those fast-walking, personally-trained gym cardholders. Most of all, I didn't want to be a blight on their adventure by slowing them down. We had that conversation, Pat and I. She assured me they were fine about taking it easier. Maybe they'd do one big hike while I was writing or whatever. Not to worry. It would all be fine. John said to pack everything I wanted to bring; there would be plenty of room. They were renting a van. We'd keep healthy snacks on hand and stop any time anybody wanted to stop. No problem. I was being so generously nurtured that my fears began to subside. Pat knows me well and knew what I needed to hear. So did John. To every pre-trip concern I voiced, the response was, "No problem."

And you know what? There were no problems! None. In fact, I look younger in the photos they took, as close to carefree as I ever look. Taking a back seat, being in charge of absolutely nothing, turned out to be quite nice. Delightful, actually.

John and Pat enjoy learning all about everything. And they graciously accept my lack of interest in overloading on facts. It was fine with them that I communed with the mighty Mississippi herself while they explored maps and narratives dedicated to rivers.

In Memphis, grief overwhelmed us at the Civil Rights Museum that includes the Lorraine Motel where Dr. King was murdered. We saw the modest little room where he visited with his colleagues before stepping out on the balcony to meet his death. The energy in the Museum was powerful. Pat relived the marches I always have regretted missing. Rosa Parks' bus was there, and so many other reminders of a courageous movement. Kids on a tour wondered aloud, "Why those two white ladies crying?"

In Santa Fe at Georgia O'Keefe's and at other museums on the trip, I wanted to absorb the paintings, internalize the color and textures. And with all the breathtaking vistas in New Mexico, I had the same feeling of wanting to breathe it all in and make it part of me.

We spent time in the magical Black Hills of South Dakota. We saw waterfalls. Mesas. Bison. Elk. Moose. We breathed the clean mountain air and hiked around Devil's Tower Monument; you saw it in "Close Encounters." We stayed at the Occidental Hotel in Buffalo, Wyoming, where we were told Butch Cassidy, Calamity Jane, and Teddy Roosevelt were regulars. At Mt. Rushmore I bought a bound copy of *The Constitution of the United States*. We were angry and sad that there were no monuments at Wounded Knee. We found the gravestones of Pat's ancestors in the lush green of Madison County, Iowa, and walked across Hogback Bridge, which we simply had stumbled upon, in the footsteps of Merrill Streep and Clint Eastwood. Truly my spirit was renewed by all that we saw and experienced.

My friends must have grown in patience from spending sixteen days in my company. And I like to think they laughed more than they might have had I not been there. I learned a lot about receiving, from the generous gift of the experience itself and all the kindnesses along the way. Pat said at some point, "I was so hoping you'd be able to allow yourself this trip." The experience turned out to be great fun, transformative even. It expanded my consciousness and unlocked something good that I still don't fully understand, that I don't need to understand.

***

One of the most sacred experiences on that trip was watching the sun rise at Chaco Canyon on the morning of Summer Solstice 2007. The electrifying energy around that ancient place gave me a sense of merging with the Great Spirit and all Creation. The feelings I had as the Native flute welcomed the sun's emergence from darkness, along with an acute awareness of my love for Pat and John, were beyond words.

We spent a good part of the day there, exploring the ruins of a Chacoan culture that had flourished in the mid-800's. [This is now Chaco Culture National Historical Park, New Mexico, a part of the National Park Service, U.S. Department of Interior.] We enjoyed a lunch of fruit, bread and cheese before the dancing began. A different tribe is invited to dance at the Solstice celebration each year, and that year the honor belonged to the Zuni. For me to sit on rocky, painfully hard ground and remain mesmerized on that very hot afternoon, you know the drumming and dancing were something special. I felt a strong connection to the culture and the place.

I knew when the trip ended John and Pat would remember all the historical facts and other information I wouldn't recall about the places we visited. I would remember looking out on that balcony at the Lorraine Motel, the faces of two happy little girls splashing in a stream at the Taos Pueblo, the "Big Sky" at 12,000 feet above sea level, and snowcaps touching clouds. The amazing Black Canyon. The eerie, beautiful Badlands. And I will never forget Solstice Sunrise at Chaco. When I get very still and call it up, memory will give me the sounds of that flute greeting the Sun.

***

The road trip with Pat and John brought yet another major sacred experience. In the Big Horn Mountains of Wyoming we visited Medicine Mountain. There, for centuries, Native Americans, even warring tribes, would gather in peace. They came to pray, connect with the Great Spirit and leave prayer offerings. Native peoples and other seekers, like us, still find solace and renewal in that sacred place. This Medicine Wheel, about 245 feet in circumference according to the brochure, has been part of Native American culture for about 10,000 years: "There are many who believe the circle is a reflection of the essence of life and that creating a circle is a sacred action."

In late June it was unthinkable to me that we would need winter jackets and hats for our pilgrimage up Medicine Mountain. Fortunately, John made sure we were "wrapped like sausages," as Pat said, hiking up the mile and a half trail, stopping regularly to catch our breath in the air 12,005 feet (2.3 miles) above sea level. We were quiet, feeling respect for the enveloping peace we sensed, even before arriving at the summit. Once at the Medicine Wheel itself, we went our separate ways, standing around the Wheel, each of us in silence. The view below was spectacular, but secondary to the sacred place where we stood that day. Prayer cloths and other offerings were tied to a rope around the great circle. I was especially moved by a small dog collar left by someone grieving the loss of his best friend.

When I felt ready to leave the Wheel, I found Pat and John sitting on a bench about a quarter of the way down. I perched on a nearby log for a minute or two, then joined them. Their faces, like mine, were tracked with tears; we embraced without a word. It felt good being in true communion. In more than one way that day, I was not alone.

Here is my favorite blessing and benediction:

> May the longtime sun
> Shine upon you,
> All love surround you,
> And the pure light within you
> Guide your way on.

Dancing on Mars

~ from a card I received long ago

***

There was a longing, especially in the early years of spiritual exploration, for my mother to understand what I was experiencing. I noticed she hadn't been giving the "accept Jesus as your Savior" talk or mentioned concern about my reservation in Hell for a long time. Dysfunction aside, there always has been extraordinary love between Mama and me. I wanted to share it all with her, wanted her to approve; wanted to "expand her horizons." At the same time, I was painfully aware that if I pushed it, I was no better than the born-again zealots who were convinced they knew what was best for me. Besides, I didn't know *what to push*. I couldn't even describe most of my feelings and experiences. When I had tried, it seemed to diminish the significance of what I was trying to communicate. As it turned out, the less I attempted to share, the more she wanted to know. Eventually Mama's questions clearly showed she was interested.

***

Although I met him only once, Ram Dass (aka Baba Ram Dass) has been a special teacher for me at various stages of my life. He was Dr. Richard Alpert, a professor at Harvard during the 1960's and made news when he was terminated for experimenting with psychedelic drugs. He traveled to India and studied there with a Hindu teacher. Ever since that time his path has been a spiritual one, and he talks about it in his first book, *Be Here Now.*

Years later he suffered a severe stroke and came through it with humility and great gratitude for many things, including his caregivers. In the aftermath of the stroke, he says he identified with his spirit rather than the physical body and focused on the love and kindness in his life. Later he wrote *Still Here,* a significant book on aging and dying. I was thrilled to attend a weekend workshop led by Ram Dass in Chapel Hill and connected, I believe, to the University of North Carolina. Ram Dass talked about how spiritual practices help us move away from identifying with the ego and toward identifying with the soul. Those words had a huge impact on me. Besides other profound teachings, there was memorable chanting, a walking meditation, and a ceremony where Ram Dass presented each of us with a sandalwood mala for prayers. Mostly I remember how courageous my mother was that weekend, not only for going with me, but for fully participating in the experience. She was totally charmed by our bald, blue-eyed leader; I was busy taking notes.

One of my favorite Ram Dass reminders: *The dance goes from realizing that you're separate (the awakening) and then to finding your way back into the totality of which you are not only a part, but which you are.*

***

On the subject of teachers, at some point I read Stephen Levine's work on death and dying, including *Who Dies?* and, *Meetings at the Edge.* And I participated in a memorable weekend workshop he taught in North Carolina. My experience there was significant because it dismantled the wall of fear surrounding my concept of "death."

I owe great thanks to the writers and workshop leaders who, in addition to the people in my everyday life, have served as my teachers. I'll be able to name only a handful of them as I reach back into memories of more than thirty years and no doubt will omit some significant ones; still, I will name those who are in my awareness today. In no particular order they are:

Coleman Barks and Rumi, Pat Rodegast and Emmanuel, Carl Jung, Ram Dass, Walt Whitman, Thich Nhat Hanh, Brook Medicine Eagle, Joan Borysenko, Belleruth Naparstek, Joseph Campbell, Hugh Prather, Pema Chodron, Wayne Dyer, David Whyte, Caroline Myss, Echart Tolle, Peace Pilgram, Louise Hay, Stephen Levine, Scott Peck, Bernie Siegel, MD, Mark Nepo, Rachel Naomi Remen, MD, Marianne Williamson, Evelyn Eaton, Black Elk, Mary Oliver, and so many others. Of course, best until last, my therapist-teacher Jack.

My love for Creator and Creation is beyond words, but mystical Persian poet Rumi comes closest to capturing it for me. His ecstatic verses are written about the "Beloved," about spiritual love of Creator, Creation, and his teacher, Shams. There are deep and delicious teachings to be found with Rumi. I delight in his sense of humor, the mischief that sparkles in his passionate profundity. My favorite poet and I share the same birthday, different century. He was born in Afghanistan on

September 30, 1207.

I once spent a special afternoon in Athens, Georgia not Greece, enjoying coffee with a friend, her friend, and her friend's friend, Coleman Barks. Poet, teacher and esteemed translator of Rumi, Coleman is an authentic person and delightful company. He gifted me with an inscribed copy of *The Essential Rumi*. The book is worn now from years of love.

From Rumi:

The breeze at dawn has secrets to tell you.
Don't go back to sleep.
You must ask for what you really want.
Don't go back to sleep.
People are going back and forth across the doorsill
where the two worlds touch.
The door is round and open.
Don't go back to sleep.

~ from *The Essential Rumi,* translated by Coleman Barks

As you can see, Rumi advocates waking up and paying attention, being fully present in, and open to, life. If you get a copy of *The Essential Rumi*, you're likely to love him, too.

***

I sent an early draft of this spiritual section to a reader-friend who said it made her want to know more: Precisely what impact certain experiences had on my personal growth, exactly what took me from Point A to Point B in my spiritual journey, and what I learned from each spiritual tradition.

Appreciative and a little frustrated by my inability to give her more concrete, linear information, I e-mailed my response. She suggested I include it in the book, so here it is:

[My journey] It's layered, overlapping, and ongoing. I can't say that I learned "A" from this particular book and that it took me to "B," where I learned something else from the Tibetan monks, or that "C," Sufism and the ecstatic love of Rumi brought me to the grounding experiences of

"D," Native American spirituality and all that I continue to learn from the natural world. It just didn't happen that way.

It's the essence of my experiences, not so much the things I learned that have expanded my spiritual awareness and my feelings of connection. There really weren't clearly-defined periods of exploration that I was "into" and "got over" or outgrew. Mostly there were experiences like the book falling at my feet, being introduced to "Emmanuel" through Callie, and hearing about this or that workshop or group or book.

[My friend had said she admired how relentless I was in my search.] I wasn't at all relentless, just open and willing to go wherever instinct guided me. I don't deserve any medals for determination. Discipline in my approach was sorely lacking; in fact, I didn't even have an approach! Nothing planned or strategized. I will sound like a stoned hippie when I say it's simply an "IS-NESS." It just is. And if I attempt to put into words that one specific thing got me to point A or Point B, it would dilute or, worse, misrepresent the magnitude and magnificence of feeling connected to "all that is." I've gotten to the point where my greatest prayer is gratitude. I probably say "thank you" at least a dozen times every day. Even for very small comforts or flashes of beauty that enrich a moment.

Thus far, this spiritual journey has been deeply rewarding. It was, and continues to be, the most energizing, exciting aspect of my life; much like falling in love, romantic love in the early stages, except it doesn't change or fade. It's an ongoing celebration I can highly recommend.

In closing, I will share my essay entitled *Namaste*:

Why is my serenity so easily lost to politicians and preachers who declare, *This is a Christian nation*? Through the lens of my mind-heart-life, I see the USA as a sanctuary for religious freedom. Freedom to subscribe to any belief or spiritual path one chooses. And the same freedom to opt out altogether.

As we approached Winter Solstice, with Christmas only days away, I was thinking about the "Christian nation" thing. How must those words make Americans of other faiths feel?

This is a magical time, celebrating the coming of Light and, for Christians, the birth of Jesus. Whether you consider Jesus an inspiring teacher of love and kindness, a personal savior, or an interesting mythological figure, this is a season of hope and happy celebrations. Or it could be, without the persistent, divisive determination to label our country "Christian."

The United States of America was founded as a safe place to believe as one chooses, to practice or not practice one's faith without fear. To me, any love-based spiritual path is a worthy one. I will respect yours, even if it's very different from mine. And I would like that same respect from you.

Hindu friends clasp their hands together prayerfully and bow in greeting as they say "Namaste." Essentially this means "I see the Divine in you." Wouldn't it be great if we could all say *Namaste* to one another and mean it?

I finally came up with an answer to, "Are you a Christian?" or, "Have you been saved?" Yes, people do get that personal in my native South. I know, it's an invasion of privacy, inappropriate at best. But if I simply respond with "not exactly" or "why do you ask?" the questioner feels compelled to "save" me or continue the inquisition. So, now I answer: "My spiritual life is too private and profound to talk about."

I was brought up in the Christian faith. However, my life and expanding world view have been enriched by other traditions over time: Buddhism, Judaism, Sufism, Native American spirituality, and other nature-based folk religions. When I study the teachings of Islam, that path is likely to offer new insights as well.

My country is not a Christian nation. It is a free nation, a spiritual melting pot, bubbling sweetly in a welcome-home kind of way. Our diversity works well unless one faith insists on being the only "right" one, unless any individual or group attempts to impose their views on everyone else.

My holiday wish, every year, is that we can agree to meet on higher ground, all of us in a garden of gratitude, to give thanks for our religious freedom. With tolerance and, even better, compassionate respect for one another, our diversity is a magnificent gift. Magnificent.

Ahhhh, yes. *Namaste.*

Part III

Home

"It is good everywhere, but home is better." ~ Yiddish saying

Home: May it mirror your passions. May it be a peaceful sanctuary for love and a benevolent guardian of memories. May it embrace you and nurture your growth.

A friend defines what's important in his life by asking, "Can it love me?" I've borrowed his approach a number of times. Most recently I asked that question about my own home. You might think I'm certifiable when I tell you that, yes, my home loves me. I can feel its comfort, its inspiration, its playful whimsy when I'm taking myself too seriously, and its peace when I need rest and rejuvenation.

Even though I understand that my true "home" exists as part of me, within me, love of a material home can be a major love relationship; one that can last a lifetime. Not really a material girl, I feel my home transcends materiality. It seems more of an organic entity than a thing. Maybe that's partly because I've loved making it the haven it is. When people tell me that certain improvements would increase its value, I find myself feeling a little, I don't know, misunderstood? It's silly, I know. The home-caring things I do and changes I make are strictly for my own comfort and enjoyment. If what I do in my home brings greater financial benefit to others when I'm no longer around, all the better. But I don't think or plan that way. I'm staying present to the gift of living in it now.

***

The home my friend Rachel built after becoming a late-life empty nester demonstrates that it's never too late to have a home you truly love. Like Rachel, Bev was able to build a home for one, with breathtaking views that bring the natural world to her every day.

Not everyone is able to build a "dream home," but home can be created in whatever space you occupy—house, condo, or apartment. Monica says her "heart feels its best" in her 600 sq. ft. 1927 vintage apartment with its cozy plant-filled porch. And Ursula, divorced after twenty-five years, was thrilled to find the bungalow that is now exclusively hers. She has turned it into a delightful space that, for the first time in her life, mirrors exactly who she is.

Making a home truly yours is an ongoing education, offering endless gifts of self-revelation. It brings opportunities for learning, and remembering, what's important to you. Like yoga, it stretches you in unimagined ways. Whether you're starting out or starting over, budget needn't stand between you and a high degree of satisfaction in your home, even if your budget is modest.

If you live alone, home is your personal canvas; you get to choose the color palette and the furnishings, the textures and the tone. If you share your living space, it's important to have your own "home within a home," a place you can create in your own image; a sanctuary where you can retreat into privacy to think, gather your wits, replenish your energy. Ideally there will be a door you can close. And open.

Home Blessing

I have a knowing
that this home
will cradle you
in peace,
soften the din
of marketplace madness
whispering *Find your center.*

I have a knowing
that this place

will embrace you
with coolness
or warmth,
whatever is needed
to balance the seasons
of your days,
to soothe,
comfort
and tenderly teach
as you allow.

Love
that sets no conditions,
holds no expectations,
flows easily

between this home
of brick and mortar
and your home
of flesh & bone.
Love nourished
by a wellspring
of truth, growing
as you breathe
in and out,
awake, fully
aware,
and celebrating
the blessings
of Home.

***

Feeling at Home

What feels like home is unique to each of us. Some thrive amid mounds of magazines and newspapers, tabletops covered with bric-a-brac. Others are happiest in a minimalist environment. Truth be told, I'd go stark-raving mad in either. Sure, sometimes I feel a tug of envy at the Zen-like simplicity of a friend's home or wish I could be okay with stepping over piles of mail and magazines. But neither would work for me. It would be like wearing shoes a size too small or too big.

Having a home I love means being fearless in making sure it's pleasing to me, not thinking of whether it will win the approval of any friend, neighbor, or relative. They won't be living there. I recommend getting brave enough to try anything, at least as far as color and furniture/object placement go. Those things can be changed fairly easily.

If, say, you paint a room "Monet Sunset" and it feels like you're stuck inside a bottle of Pepto Bismol when it's done, hurry back to the paint store! Paint can be pricy, but for the significant difference it makes, it's worth whatever it costs. Color is key to making a space uniquely one's own.

Color cards from paint stores can be helpful. Using the copier, one friend has enlarged a few she especially liked, masking-taped them to the wall and lived with them for a while before making a decision.

I'm fond of fabric stores where I'm allowed to bring home, and keep, small samples of appealing material. Never mind that I don't sew. It's all about how the colors, textures, and patterns make me feel. Fabric swatches help me choose the colors and designs I want to have surrounding me.

In making changes at home, I did myself a favor by giving up perfectionism. Striving for "the perfect" inevitably leads to analysis paralysis where I'm frozen in obsession, endlessly weighing options. I remind myself and you: Trust your instincts. Build self-trust with every decision you make, and celebrate each small success. For me, a decorating project or purchase is a huge success if it makes me feel really good once it's part of the household. When I'm not too entrenched in an idea of what I want, whatever I need is more likely to find me. And I'm likely to love it. It's all about staying open and aware.

Of course the equation changes if you're sharing space, especially with someone whose tastes are vastly different. If need be, you can always call in a "decorating coach" to help find a good compromise. Many designers are willing to consult on an hourly basis to resolve specific problems. Or you might arrive at the solution you need by recruiting a friend to brainstorm with the two of you and serve as a mediator. Living solo or partnered, don't torture yourself and spoil the fun by making molehills into mountains.

***

If you don't know what feeling truly "at home" means for you, wouldn't you like to find out? If so, you might begin noticing how you feel in other people's homes. If you are especially relaxed or suddenly energized, ask yourself whether the surroundings are affecting your mood. Can you identify what triggered the feeling?

Over time I discovered that my spirit needs cheerful, nurturing surroundings. Some traditional furnishings and warm wood tones are important for a sense of security. They seem to "ground" me. A couple of family heirlooms give me a sense of life as a continuum. They connect me to my roots. Some dramatic touches reflect and feed my passion, and there's some whimsey to make me smile every day. Examples would be the bodacious mermaid painted on an old shutter and "The Grapes of Laugh" featuring three of my favorite things: laughter, wine, and a crow. I need warm, bright color and candles, always. Soft lighting for ambience and good, focused light for reading. Of course a comfortable place to sit and to sleep are bottom-line basic. And art and special photographs that please me are a must, as well. Last Christmas I gave myself an electric fireplace insert; it's amazingly realistic. Puts out minimal heat but adds the ambient warmth I wanted.

I'm no expert at feng shui, but a friend who is reminded me that bedrooms are for peaceful rest and intimacy. No electronics. No bill-paying therein. No work. There's a battery-operated brass clock at my bedside rather than digital; no TV. Sometimes I do cheat and allow Happy, my laptop, into bed for writing, as I am doing now. When writing or editing begins to feel like work, I'll head to the desk.

Maybe describing a room would illustrate the art of the possible when it comes to creating spaces in sync with who you are. Telling you about one of my own rooms might show that getting the look, the feeling, you want in a room or a house can be done without spending a lot of money.

Welcome to my bedroom: A four-panel Japanese screen owns the wall opposite my bed; it's an original, painted by an artist in Kyoto. A signature chop is imprinted in the left-hand corner of the golden hues that underlie bamboo trees and flowers blooming in deep orange and white; there's a little bird nearby deciding on his next move. That I was drawn to this screen was surprising. Oriental art never has been a favorite. Had it not been in a thrift store, I wouldn't have given it a second look, probably wouldn't have noticed it at all. This original art would be worth no telling what in a gallery or status store. I've seen similar screens, prints not half as lovely as this original, for over $500. And for what became the centerpiece of my bedroom, the golden, sun-washed beauty I see when I open my eyes each morning, I paid $30. I cherish the serenity I feel looking at it.

There are gems out there waiting for you, too. It's just a matter of looking around, sometimes in unlikely places, and returning often to benefit from rapid inventory turnover at low-cost consignment and thrift stores. The screen was a lesson in staying open to change and having the willingness to revisit my preferences. They have evolved over time, changed as I have changed.

Quite a few household treasures have come from thrift or consignment stores, flea markets, and garage sales. In the weeks after the screen came to live in my bedroom, a beautiful Paprika silk comforter called to me from a red-dot clearance bin at World Market. I was able to get the comforter and matching pillow shams for under $60. Had been over $200.

At the double windows are white paper shades and sheers in two tones of striped cream, a pattern reminiscent of bamboo. They soften and lighten the room. Understand, I didn't know they would serve such a purpose when I saw them. I got them because I liked the way they look.

Under the windows is a narrow, distressed wooden bench in medium green built by a local craftsman. I found it at a resale store at the beach. At this moment the bench holds a meditating Buddha (about the size of an accent lamp), books, and a small vase of flowers. I always enjoy fresh flowers or greenery in my room. I've loved and lived with my Buddha ever since I saw him in an antiques, collectibles and junk co-op probably fifteen years ago. (At the same place a few years later, I found an African drum with a face mask carved in the base for $30. Too high-energy for the bedroom, but it's a star in the living area.) Atop a few books lying down next to Buddha is a brass bird I call "Buddha's bird." The day I received it as a gift I had no idea what I would do it. I love birds, real ones, but.... Now he's precious to me as the friend who gave it. It all comes together in time.

Under the screen is a simple, narrow sofa table from Goodwood and stained by me. I remember my friend Pat would not be defeated the day she took me to pick it up. She willed it to fit in her car and, miraculously, it obliged. It holds, at one end, a lamp and a little gold and natural straw letter basket, perfect with the screen and lamps, was fifty cents at a thrift store. At the other end, a framed picture of my granddaughter playing dress-up, a small bronze mermaid, and a candle. There's a golden-brown wicker rocking chair with a cushion and throw pillow next to the end of the table where the lamp is. A small cane-bottom chair that belonged to my grandmother is at the table, with a big basket holding magazines underneath. A majesty palm is happy near the windows at the end of the bench. The palm relates to the bamboo on the screen, the lucky bamboo plant, and the pattern in the sheers. Matching traditional bedside tables were my mother's; they hold brass lamps, different designs from different times and places, on either side of the cherry sleigh bed, queen-size. A corner hat rack is home for my beach hats and a bike helmet I've never worn for biking, but keep in anticipation of a tornado warning. There's a second large basket in the room, holding books under my bedside table. Reading material is close at hand everywhere in the house.

In "Return to Eden," the framed poster over my bed, a man and woman who could be Mayans have found sanctuary in a garden with huge yellow hibiscus blossoms and palm fronds. They sit close together, heads touching at the temples. They are sleeping, their faces radiating innocence and peace. I found "Eden" at a consignment store, framed, for $12.

On the narrow wall between a pair of white louvered closet doors are three dark frames hanging in a vertical row; two are shadowboxes. One is a collage I was inspired to make while corresponding with an artist, exchanging my poems and pictures of his artistic creations electronically. In the collage are lush green images, an ancient wooden door, lines from a poem I wrote, words from Rumi, and a large, rustic key. That collage is my best memory of a short-lived relationship, lovely in the pen-pal stage. Another frame holds three very old keys whose history I don't know. Must have been a bargain. Last in the trio is a framed postcard, a charming village in Italy, sent by a friend visiting there.

The walls in my bedroom are a soft yellow. There's no overhead lighting, just a vintage white ceiling fan that came with the house.

I like to incorporate the five elements in a room whenever possible. In this case there's Earth with the palm, bamboo, and cut flowers. Fire is symbolized by the orange comforter, shams, tabletop candle, orange flowers in the Japanese screen and Eden poster. Metal is in a vase, the brass lamps, and light switch plate. The furniture and the carving of the lovers represent wood. Water? Of course there's water in the flower vase and bamboo, but, best of all, there's the beautiful lake I can see from the bedroom windows.

There are good memories associated with many items in the room and the love of friends and family in objects they've given me. My granddaughter lives too far away, and photos make it easier to feel closer to her. That's a lot of detail, but bear with me.

If you're fairly clear on who you are or willing to get clear, I know you can create a home that reflects who you are. A home that makes you feel very, very good when you walk through the door. So good you might be reluctant leave.

Go slowly. It all takes time, and it would spoil the fun if you did it all in a hurry. It's fun to add things as you go along: souvenirs from travels, special art that finds you, gifts from people you love. If you want immediate change but can't manage a large project for now, choose one corner in one room—a new table or lamp, or a painting you might consider moving from one place to another. You might be surprised by the impact a small change can make.

I've found it's important to keep my surroundings up to date. I'm not talking about trends here. For me, updating means checking in with myself periodically to see whether this or that item or aspect still has meaning. For example: Does it still make me feel good? Is it comfortable, functional? You might ask yourself whether the colors on your walls are the ones you need at the present time. Maybe you've gotten over the monochromatic look and would enjoy living with more or different colors. Sometimes it's good to take a *how much do I love this or that aspect of my home* inventory.

Here's an inventory example from my own experience. At some point I bought a poster-size print of a little girl, maybe 6 or 7, standing beside a brass-potted hydrangea. The girl had red hair, and the light in the painting was exquisite. I splurged to have it framed beautifully. It was perfect for my dining room. After some time passed, I began to look at the painting less and, when I did, it was with a twinge of sadness. Indeed, the girl's face was sad as she stood there in her starched white dress, knowing she must be careful not to get dirty. She seemed to be staring into the middle distance. Sometimes I'd look at the portrait and feel angry. Angry! What was that about? It was a nice painting. I had liked it enough to buy it not long ago, hadn't I?

Finally, I understood that the girl might have been me as a young girl, me throughout most of my life, poised for action when cued by one of the people I lived to please. And, like me, ever apart from the rough and tumble world of fearless children. Staring at the little girl I could hear echoes from the past, " Be sure to get home before dark! Are you dressed for Sunday School?" Like this girl, I was always "standing by" on the periphery of others' lives, waiting.

Exploring my feelings about that painting was the beginning of saying goodbye to that passive, people-pleasing aspect of myself and to the little girl in me who was weaned on fear. The experience helped me see that I still was giving fear too much power in my life. Waking up to that truth has been a significant part of my growth. It's all about awareness and what we do with our "seeing" once awakened to a new aspect of our own truth.

I took some quiet time to honor the sad, fearful girl I had been, and then I let her go. I donated the print to a charity shop. Later, I painted a bright, bodacious abstract to go in that frame.

***

Sidebar: Recently I've gotten lazy about entertaining. I sometimes entertain myself with thoughts of entertaining, coming up with new menus and recipes, then give up the idea when it's time to consider the guest list. But a high school friend inspired me recently, and I might even follow through next time.

Marsha feels fortunate to be living in her childhood home. She loves having plants around and feeding the hungry bird-friends who visit her garden. She also enjoys feeding her large extended family at Christmas and at least once during the summer. Her kitchen is small, an unchangeable fact since she has chosen to maintain the integrity of the original structure. Marsha is an example of using unbounded imagination to come up with solutions to apparent limitations.

She wanted her big family to share a special meal with her, and she wanted everyone, including herself, to spend time having fun together afterwards, not working at cleanup. She also said "no" to paper plates. Marsha doesn't mind doing the dishes later, says she enjoys the tear-down phase of a party. So, she has her guests rinse plates and silverware at the kitchen sink and place them in two dish pans filled with hot sudsy water— in her bathtub! It gets the mess out of sight until the party's over and she's ready to deal with cleanup. "Everybody knows the drill now, and it makes entertaining easy," she says.

***

My current home is not the first significant home-love of my life. In the South Carolina Midlands I lived in a well-loved home for twenty years. I said many times that the only way I'd leave it would be "feet first." A lot of life was lived there. Son Neal shared that home with me during some tough teenage years. My two dogs lived and died there. It was a place treasured friends felt comfortable bringing their tears and laughter. I had opened myself to the possibility of a "love" relationship there, and it was there I began coming to terms with my solitary life.

The house was on a beautiful street across from a lake. I could see a sliver of the lake from the big shadowbox window in the kitchen, could see more in winter when the trees were bare. Mine was a small house in a neighborhood of increasingly huge, expensive homes. People across the way had torn down a charming, spacious house and replaced it with the most ostentatious piece of real estate you ever saw. It was far too big for the lot; I half expected it to sink into the water. The house screamed "nouveau riche" and completely screwed up my postage-stamp view of the lake. I now faced a wrought iron fence topped out with spears; it spoiled the peaceful landscape.

Then the house next door to that one was sold and gutted. In that case, the one they demolished could have made *Architectural Digest*. Old money this time, but still it wasn't as nice as the house they ruined. As my mother would say, "Some people have more money than taste." My older neighbors had died out and taken all the good taste with them.

Understand, I loved my familiar city and the longtime friends and happy acquaintances who live there. I liked the location, about ten minutes from my downtown office, three minutes from a wonderful shopping area. Not a behemoth mall, but a shopping center with great restaurants, a fantastic Fresh Market, ice cream parlor, and Hallmark Shop; also, a book store, post office, Chico's and Steinmart. The public library was within walking distance. Perfect!

So why in the world did I decide to move? I fell in love, that's why.

***

I was looking at the real estate section in the Sunday paper, keeping an eye out for a place that might work for my friend Elizabeth. Somehow I wandered into "resort property" and saw an ad that peaked my curiosity. A "for sale by owner" described a Lowcountry town house only a short drive from my favorite beach—such a special place that son Neal has said he plans to scatter my ashes there. The puzzling part of the ad was that one of the amenities was a "pavilion" at the beach. I had no idea what was meant by "pavilion" in the context of the town house ad or where it might be. The beach is on a little island that guards its noncommercial charm as carefully as my grandmother guarded her pearls. We usually spent our summer vacations there when I was growing up. My parents met on the island and danced at the same pavilion where I would dance as a teenager. But that pavilion burned to the ground long ago.

A couple of Sundays later I was back into the real estate listings, ostensibly for Elizabeth's benefit, and the ad was still there. So, I decided to call the ad-placer on Monday and satisfy my curiosity.

He told me the "pavilion at the beach" was a clubhouse for homeowners of his community. It had a big common room, kitchen, bathrooms, screened porch and deck. No bedrooms. And where was it, across the main highway, off the island? Actually it was on the oceanfront! When he described the location, I knew exactly where he meant.

In a matter of minutes this man and I were like long-lost friends. All the while I was assuring him I couldn't buy his town house, even though it sounded lovely. That was in early April. He was lamenting the fact that he and his wife had needed to leave their Lowcountry paradise to care for their parents upstate. Before the conversation ended, he suggested I drive down just for fun, have a look. His wife would be there the following weekend, and the azaleas should be in full bloom.

So I invited my mother to come with me on Saturday. I promised a picnic and the azaleas, not that she needed any arm-twisting to support me in satisfying my curiosity.

***

We had a perfect day for our day trip and no problem finding the property. Driving under a canopy of giant, moss-draped oaks, I was surprised to find myself blinking away tears. I got chill-bumps. It was as if I knew this place, had been here long ago. I heard myself saying, "I think I want to live here." In my body, deep in my solar plexus, it felt like I was coming home instead of being there for the first time.

Long story not quite so long, we met my phone pal's wife, Alice, and I assured her once again I couldn't afford their place. They had a spectacular view though, a lake with cypress trees growing in it. I felt great tenderness for those trees, and I was mesmerized by the water.

The lush landscape was ablaze with azaleas, the magnolias loaded with waxy white flowers. As we made our way toward the other on-site clubhouse, another fragrance, jasmine, sweetened the air. Alice was so gracious I wished I could afford their large town home.

After saying our goodbyes, I contacted a real estate agent, "just curious" to know if there were any smaller units we could see as long as we were there. And yes, there was one three-bedroom available. The listed price was dramatically lower than the four-bedroom we had just seen.

Because of the price, I assumed there wouldn't be a water view, and I wouldn't be interested. I was feeling a little downhearted about that when the agent drove us to the available town house. It was in the same building we'd just visited! The view was almost the same. Here there was not only a close-up view of the lake, but the Intracoastal Waterway was visible, too! When a sailboat glided by, I realized I was hopelessly in love, the way one might be with a person.

You know the song "What I Did for Love" from *A Chorus Line*? That's where I was.

***

Even when the "honeymoon" ended, I was still in love. The town house was in terrible shape. Not structurally, but it needed serious aesthetic rehab. Some of the changes would be costly, so I'd need to sell my home in Columbia for as much as possible. That way I could create something wonderful inside the townhouse, something worthy of the beauty outside the windows.

I had taken a leap of faith and given the agent a $300 check as earnest money. It was the agent's first day in the real estate business. Bright and early Monday morning he called to say he had no idea how much money he should have asked for on Saturday, then told me what the owner would accept. I sent the check that day.

I'll skip the harrowing detailed negotiations and all the roadblocks that came after that, not to mention the *true hell* of selling my house and negotiating both deals without an agent. Once the condo was mine, I began a budget-friendly home makeover. I was commuting three hours each way from my longtime, now "for sale," home. At the Lowcountry town house I had an on-loan air mattress, a floor lamp, ladder, boom box, bistro table and two chairs, and a cooler for perishables. Fortunately, red wine and cereal bars required no refrigeration. Mostly, I was painting, and on two occasions there was a willing friend to help.

The look on my friend Jodie's face when she applied the first stroke of paint to the wall in the living room was unforgettable. The paint was yella. She hesitated, then asked, "Was this the color you had in mind?"

I had bought three gallons and made an instant decision that I was going to love it, regardless. "It is now," I said, and the transformation was under way. Jodie worked so fiercely that weekend that she went home with a dreadful case of tendonitis. I still feel twinges of guilt. Nevertheless, the yellow in the living area, almost shocking in bright daylight, offers warmth and comfort, especially at night and on cloudy days. It feels as if the sun is pouring through me. I need that, especially in winter. As Van Gogh said, "Yellow is capable of charming God." And me, too.

***

I was doing whatever painting I could and making critical decisions with the amazing man who was ripping out the carpet, taking down a kitchen cabinet, installing new countertops and flooring, and a dozen other things to make my new home livable. John allowed nothing to defeat him, and I never heard him complain. Never. He continues to have my utmost respect and gratitude. After accomplishing whatever I could there, I would drive back to the Midlands to work at selling the Columbia house. A bridge loan that scared hell out of me was the primary motivation for pushing so hard at both places.

The "new" town house had been rented for a few years before the owner decided to sell. The carpet was three shades of brown and beige, perfect for the office of a color-blind used car salesman. No carpet in all of history could have been that ugly. John saved a small sample for future show and tell, just in case anyone might accuse me of exaggerating.

I was alone at the new town house over July Fourth weekend with the determined intention of painting all three bedrooms in three days. The name my mother later gave the place, Tranquility, wouldn't have fit at that time. On the last marathon painting day I heard voices downstairs and stood at the stairwell listening. Must have left the door unlocked earlier. I knew no one there. I knew no one anywhere who would walk into my home uninvited, much less without ringing the bell. I heard a man's voice saying to a woman who agreed with him, "These colors surely are loud!"

Paintbrush in hand, I headed down the stairs faster than I knew was possible. Completely exhausted, clothes and matted hair spattered with paint, wearing no makeup whatsoever, I was about to meet my neighbors. A short man with a really bad hairpiece and a woman in baggy Bermudas stood next to a cocker spaniel in what would become my dining room.

I was pissed. "I believe the word you meant to use is vibrant." This was not the day to mess with me. I didn't appreciate their barging in and, insult to injury, bringing a dog in without asking. I love dogs, but I wasn't happy about the boundary violation. Still, my Southern Belle attitude kicked in just enough to take the sharper edges off the hostility.

The curious neighbor had no clue he had offended me. My snapping-turtle attitude didn't faze him. He was too busy going on about a spaghetti supper, explaining that he was on the Social Committee. There's a Social committee, *Omygod noooo*! That visit was the beginning of a hero's journey to claim my new home, my privacy, and indeed my new life. I was planning to stake a claim on my version of Walden Pond and honor, or at least humor, the introvert I've kept in hiding while living the life of an extrovert. The introvert was making big changes to create an authentic life. My plan was that it be well lived, in peace and privacy. (Turns out I would grow to love my neighbors. No doubt some of them think my lack of interest in social events is odd, and they probably consider me odd. Yet they are unfailingly kind and respectful about how I choose to live my life in our corner of Eden.)

By the way, the high point of that weekend came the night of the Fourth. When it became too dark to paint, I opened a bottle of wine, and put some cold supper on a paper plate. As I seated my weary self at the little bistro table overlooking the water, a fireworks display began, as if on cue, the minute I lifted my glass. The pyrotechnics were coming from the other side of the lake, magnificently reflected in the water. I'd never seen anything like it, other than a few orchestrated by professionals for big events. I toasted my unknown benefactors for this delightful surprise, and later lifted a glass to freedom, just before sinking into the air mattress. I was feeling enormous peace and gratitude when sleep took over for the remainder of the night.

***

Just as I put my Columbia house on the market, the owner of the vacant lot behind me had it graded. That caused my yard to flood when it rained. Twice, there was a "river" rushing through at such velocity it forced the gate open, swept away lawn chairs, and left a slimy, inch-thick residue in the back yard and driveway. I remember going out in a rainstorm one Sunday night to take down the "For sale by owner" sign. Water in the driveway was ankle deep. That was a meltdown moment, one in which I felt utterly alone.

The flooding issue finally was resolved, but there were some harrowing weeks leading to resolution. Ultimately the owner of the lot behind me became my home buyer. That was a good thing, but it would have been easier on my nervous system if I'd been able to sell a lot sooner. The uncertainties and the pressure of a bridge loan had been tough.

Packing a lifetime of belongings was a task I underestimated. At some point I did a "giveaway" in the Native American tradition. At various times friends stopped by to choose an item or items from my "letting go" bounty, including a mini-library. I consigned a few pieces of furniture and sold lawn equipment, tools, and my porch rockers to friends. I donated other items to a local shelter.

One day my mother brought her handyman to clear the attic and my storage house out back. How I thought I could pack the entire house myself is beyond me. Most of my local friends were either dealing with work-related pressures or away for summer vacation. And I'm always reluctant to ask for help. I was honored that two friends wanted to host farewell parties before the move, but I declined the offers. No time. Must focus.

I had asked my childhood friend Vicki to drive down and share my first night at "Tranquility." I wanted her to help me celebrate this milestone in my life. The next day would be her birthday, and she'd need to return to Columbia for a family celebration. I made a mental note to get a cake which turned out to be a big brownie with candles.

Even though my friend Cora was working long hours on a grant proposal with a hard deadline, she gave me two evenings of packing help. Betty packed several boxes, as well. Earlier, Paula had taken pictures for my "for sale by owner" flyer and measured square footage of the house. Brother D had helped put the brochure together and later packed my computer for the move. And I thought I could do the rest. Actually, I did do most of "the rest" myself.

Just two days before the move, I learned that lamps, paintings, etc. would need to be boxed, so I decided to hire packers for a couple of hours to deal with heavier, more awkward items. It was an expense I didn't need, but I booked them anyway. I was exhausted, "running on empty."

An earache kept me awake most of the night before the packers were to come; Betty sat with the packers while I went to a "doc in a box." I left a check for her to pay the guys in case they finished before I returned.

I waited nearly two hours to see a doctor, then waited at the pharmacy for ear drops. The packers had just left when I got back to the house. They had spent most of the time packing canned goods and spices I hadn't even planned to take with me! Each small item had been wrapped more carefully than my glasses and stemware; most of the big items were still there for me to pack. I surrendered to the situation, took a deep breath and got busy.

***

There was no sleep again that night. I had loaded every inch of the car, so there was only room for my handbag and me when the movers arrived early next morning. My mid-July moving day would turn out to be the hottest of the year so far. Before I knew it, I heard one of the movers say, "We're closing the doors now; the truck is full." I was stunned. This was surreal. That couldn't be! What about all the stuff on the front porch? "There's no more room."

What to do? The driver had started the engine. They had directions to my new place, but I needed to be there when they arrived. It was okay, they said; they'd be getting a drive-through burger, and I could catch up with them on the road. They were cool. I was near hysteria.

A call to Vicki saved me. She would come by the house and get everything on the porch. I couldn't see how. She said I'd be surprised what that her wagon, Ava Audi would hold. And also by what she could lift. Yes, I would be surprised, and I still was worried about her back. Not to worry; just be safe. She'd see me later.

That I was safe was a miracle of the highest order. I was totally wiped out from two nights with almost no sleep and only a cereal bar for fuel. I was too tired to be sentimental as I backed out of the driveway that had been mine for twenty years. Good thing I had said my goodbyes to Casita Lucinda earlier in the week.

I did catch up to the movers, after driving sixty miles in low gear without noticing.

***

The movers and I arrived in tandem and walked into my townhouse. The air conditioning had gone out, and it was hotter than dog's breath. I couldn't imagine these two guys hauling my furniture in and up the stairs in the suffocating heat. I called the property manager for a number of someone who might get it going again, and soon a young fellow named Ken was crawling around under the house. Later, he drove into town to get a part. I visualized his safe return.

The movers were good sports, wringing wet as they went about getting the job done. And get it done they did. I kept handing out water and insisting they drink up, telling myself these guys were young and fit. Not vulnerable to heat stroke. They got my bed set up as well as the guest bed for Vicki. Those were my top priorities. As the two men and their truck were about to go, I gave them each twenty bucks. They were delighted, probably because tipping was prohibited. Actually, they deserved a lot more. I doubted they would be paid what they deserved for literally taking the heat and maintaining good humor in the process.

After they were gone, I foraged in my handbag for the ear drops. Then the search was on for the box of bed linens.

Vicki and Ken arrived at the same time. Her car was overflowing with my belongings, and we unloaded immediately. She had gotten everything off the porch. I was immensely relieved and grateful beyond words. We agreed that I'd do a couple of things upstairs while she ran the vacuum downstairs. Then, Hallelujah, we would sit down and have a drink.

While I was making the guest room bed, all the smoke alarms began to go off. What? This was what fate had in store, a damned fire? I ran outside to ask Ken whether I should call 911. I called his name until he crawled from under the house. Said he'd been testing something or other and assured me everything was okay, just a little motor odor. He was drenched.

Soon the air was running. Vicki was sipping her bourbon, and I poured a glass of wine after locating my checkbook. Between stress, sleep deprivation, and the earache, I didn't have the energy to worry about the cost of the repair. My old friend and I stood over the cooling vents, giddy with relief.

Ken came in to present his bill, apologizing that he was dirty. He was assured that we had no problem with dirty heroes. But he was welcome to wash up, if he'd like, and join us for a glass of wine. Wine was all I had to offer. He was about to refuse, but his face lighted up when Vicki announced she had some bourbon. The three of us sat around the table on the sun porch, and all the cares of the day, and the week, the months, began to fade away.

With a good friend and a halfway good bottle of Cabernet, I can get through most anything.

***

Looking back, it's hard to believe I lived through that whole buying-selling-moving process. The way it happened had to be, as Neal would say, "a God thing," or fate, whatever you want to call it. There's no other explanation for my instant love of the place, the willingness to change my life completely, and finding the courage to take some scary risks. There's no doubt in my mind that I'm where I'm meant to be and as much in love as I was the first day I saw "Tranquility."

I remember standing on the front porch my second night here and thinking it was the darkest place I'd ever been. Then I realized for the first time, I didn't know anyone here. And I felt remarkably okay about that, not alone or lonely in the least.

Now, six years later, when stars are dancing in the night sky, when the Moon lingers over her reflection in the lake, when the egrets fly home at twilight, when a lazy gator glides by and a breeze stirs the sea grasses and teases the Spanish moss in the cypress trees, nothing else matters. I'm wide awake, fully present in my life and living it with great love and gratitude. I'm dancing on Mars, and all is well.

Egrets Flying Home

She likes to pretend
these birds could fly
on one wing
in their easy feathers,
white innocence
airborne.

They fly, one by one,
high in the evening air
as sky-fire lingers
long enough for the
elegant pilgrimage home,
for cypress divas
to wave their Spanish hair
bidding them goodnight.

An unseen face
watches from the big window
each day,
watches as they travel
from lower lake or bay,
smiling them toward
piney grove destination
with love outrageous and
profound.

O, Great Egret do you know
your splendor?

One...two...three now
flying into shadow...
a few long moments before
the fourth glides by,
soon the fifth...and sixth.
Finally the last straggler,
surely the optimist hoping

for one more fish,
in a hurry now and black
against what's left of the light.
Cypress shadows merge
with lake
as the love behind the window
takes soft pleasure in knowing
they're all home now.

She switches on the reading lamp
and decides
her favorite number is seven.

Part IV

Notes from a Recovering Victorian

Many centuries ago, the story goes, a woman consulted with the moon about not having slept with a man for several years; the Moon said it had been far longer for her, but she didn't believe she was missing very much.

Those words might also have been expressed by women in my grandmother's generation and beyond. Case in point: My mother's "Aunt Ellie" married a minister who looks in faded photos as if a smile would shatter his solemn face. When asked whether she loved her husband, Aunt Ellie answered without hesitation, "Not at night."

The couple's eight children are evidence that the reverend believed in sex. But I'm thinking he might not have excelled in the art of lovemaking.

From what I understand, marital sex often was considered just another chore in those days. It was to be borne stoically, like childbirth. Back then, if you heard the old mattress creaking deep in the night you'd hope he wouldn't be reaching for you. You were exhausted. But you were supposed to be there if he wanted you. And if, every time he reached out, there was a strong chance you'd be getting another baby, how turned on would you be?

'Sex as marital duty' relates to the thinking that women "belonged" to their husbands, just a piece of, well, real estate. The women-as-property craziness has lessened over time, as we've wised up and fought it. But the attitudes of Aunt Ellie's generation didn't vanish with my grandmother's and not entirely with my mother's. After all, even in "her day," the 1940's and 50's, birth control methods were still undependable. My mother had four babies and no pill to prevent unintended pregnancy. Condoms were, still are, far from fail-safe. My grandmother's pre-marital lecture to my mother was short, if not sweet: "If your husband touches you on your wedding night, he is no gentleman." Now that was a happy sendoff!

I learned as much about sex from what the women in my life didn't say as from things they said: *Men were supposed to like sex; that's just how they were. Their wives only pretended to like it.* Attitudes about sex have been passed down in our family for generations, along with the superstitions and the silverware. The ancestral fears took up residence in me long before I even knew for sure what sex was. Later, a free-floating anxiety would seep into my pores any time the subject was mentioned.

While some female relatives appear to share my longtime repression,

I think a couple have taken the fast track in the opposite direction. I sometimes wonder whether they are consciously compensating for our inability to live as sexual adventurers. I also wonder whether these happy wanderers got free passes in some twilight-zone lottery, while the card I got said "Do not pass go."

***

A role model for authenticity and the sexual art-of-the-possible came along when I was about forty. Eva became my aunt by marrying my father's oldest brother. She was in her sixties then; he was closer to seventy. It was a second marriage, after first marriages ended with the death of their spouses. Eva's invalid husband had been in her dutiful care for nearly a decade before he died.

Eva and Uncle Ed lived in Florida and sometimes paid a visit on their way to the North Carolina mountains. I felt a connection the first time I met Eva, trusted her instantly. Later, I realized it was her authenticity I was sensing. She was warm, likable, and obviously comfortable in her own skin. She was who she was, the real deal.

After that first meeting she sent what would become one of my favorite books, *The Education of Little Tree* by Forrest Carter. She inscribed it, "I'm glad we're kindred." So was I.

It was a joy seeing Eva and Ed together. Besides their strong chemistry, mutual love and respect fairly radiated from them. They had grabbed the brass ring of a second chance and never let go. Ed had plenty of money, so they were able to travel the world, play lots of golf, and enjoy good times with friends and family. Years later, Eva loved Ed through his struggle with cancer. And when he died, she grieved the loss of her sweetheart deeply.

Rather than go down for the funeral, I promised to visit when things got too quiet around her house. And I did that. We had a wonderful time sharing confidences, tears, and belly laughs. She told me their love story, adding, "Never believe you're too old to fall in love and have a fabulous, intimate, sexy life. We just need to get more creative about sex as we get older."

She was comfortable with her sexuality, a "first" for me to observe. I had cringed watching some women her age convince themselves they were still in their twenties. I felt embarrassed for them when they made fools of themselves.

It was not at all that way with Eva. I think the difference was that she wasn't confused about who she was. Eva was fully aware of who she was and comfortable about being the age she was. You could see her confidence in the way she moved her body and the way she dressed, feminine and tastefully sexy, into her eighties. She didn't allow an aging body to sabotage her sexuality. And, as long as she lived Eva, continued to own her personal power.

If only she had been in my life during my teens and twenties! I wonder whether her early influence might have altered my attitudes about sex. I also wonder whether I'd have grown into my own authenticity much sooner. Of course I'll never know for sure, but I'm leaning in favor of *yes* and *yes.*

***

Although I didn't take an active part in the women's movement, I admired the dedicated activists on the front lines. Still do. I'm grateful for their courage and the hard work they did for all of us. These women built a platform and stood firmly on it, insisting that our gender receive equal treatment under the law. Around that time there was a shift in the way we thought about sex. We wanted it to be good for us, too. Unlike our grandmothers, we began to expect that our voices be heard in the bedroom as well as the board room.

During the Sixties the fear of pregnancy became less acute, thanks to the advent of "the pill." But fear and anxiety continued to live in the tension between doing whatever it took to "get and keep your man" and whether, if you surrendered your virginity, you'd still be loved and respected.

More women relaxed about sex before marriage though, you know, deciding "not to buy the car without a test-drive." Yet some of the young women I knew remained deeply conflicted about that, thanks to the pre-feminist culture often glorified in the South, along with our mothers' and grandmothers' endless admonitions. Losing their approval was unthinkable, for me at any rate. In my corner of the world most of us still cared mightily about what people thought of us, especially the significant older women in our lives.

Growing up, I internalized the disapproval expressed, in cold stares and scalding words, about women who wore skirts too short or blouses that strained at the buttons. Of course the ones with strained buttons had big breasts like mine, so that added to fuel to my burning self-consciousness and shame.

I'll never forget an older relative I respected exclaiming that she'd just seen a neighbor riding a bicycle *in a skirt. Yes, it covered her knees, but still....* Apparently the bike rider committed yet another offense, *she was wearing a ribbon in her hair, that hair was longer than it ought to be at her age ... acts like she's a teenager, and her husband not gone a year! Shameful.*

That judgmental commentary was disturbing to me for several reasons. Most of all, my gut told me the assessment wasn't fair. I knew this woman came from "a good family," generally meaning that her family had lived in our town for generations and managed to keep their dirty linen in the family. I knew the woman was a widow, raising her children alone. The loss of the family breadwinner had meant she needed to join the work force. I had admired her in a way, yet I was little conflicted after the harsh criticism for what I saw as minor infractions. How bad could hair ribbons and bike-riding be? I began to question my opinion of this independent woman, and then felt ashamed of myself for questioning. I was more uncertain than ever about which behaviors and appearances were acceptable in the eyes of the women whose acceptance I so needed. I needed it because I was a long way from accepting myself then. Even in my confusion, I was a little annoyed by the criticism. Now I wonder how the woman even found time to take a bike ride, busy as she was trying to make ends meet and raising children, not to mention dealing with becoming a widow at thirty-something. In her case, poetic justice was at work: She became a very successful businesswoman, breaking sales records long before there were traveling saleswomen in our area. I imagine her success in "a man's world" subjected her to further criticism.

The biking-neighbor critique had evolved into a conversation about "those kinds of women." I paid close attention in my struggle to understand exactly how the critics defined "those kind." I wanted to be sure I didn't become one. I wasn't at all clear about where the "attractive girl" and "trashy girl" lines were drawn.

More than once I was reminded that men only want one thing. Mothers, aunts, and grandmothers would say anything to scare off a scandal. And maybe sometimes they were trying to protect us. I remember lectures, triggered by the gossip of the day or just out of the blue, for no reason I could detect. Once under way, Mama's lectures on the urgency of my being a "nice girl" were pretty predictable. I heard repeatedly that it would "kill" Mammy and Mama if something happened. "If something happened" meant getting pregnant or being involved in anything that might result in embarrassment to the family.

Any wonder I'm still a little rigid about rule-following? That works well in the context of, say, filing tax returns on time or submitting queries or manuscripts according to publishers' requirements. I no longer care, however, whether someone judges my appearance, or the way I live my life. I hold fast to the belief that what someone thinks of me is none of my business. Because it isn't!

I wish I'd had it in me, as a girl and young woman, to speak my mind and enjoy shocking the more puritanical people in my orbit. As a girl and as a younger woman, I wanted more than anything to believe Rhett Butler: *With enough courage you can do without a reputation.* Even with the passage of time and my hard-won growth, I haven't been able to adopt Captain Butler's words as my personal mantra. But I'm getting closer.

Today my candor still surprises some of the peripheral people in my life. As I've said before, I generally say what I mean and mean what I say these days, and I try not to say it mean. I keep forgetting that "telling it like you see it" can be stunning, especially here in the South.

***

Today I consider the warnings of women in the family, and the culture in general, a form of emotional blackmail: they'd literally "die" if I made one mistake? Then I'd better be very careful. Always. In the midst of the relentless judgments and random moralizing that fell on my ears, there was also conflicting talk. Most of the talk came from neighbors, friends of my grandmother's, and more distant relatives. Mama and Mammy never were inclined to trash other people. Neither was Papa, for that matter.

As mentioned earlier, "the talk" sometimes revolved around a theme of making oneself seductively attractive to "get a man" or hang on to one. It seemed terribly important to do that. I was involved in serious conversations relating to "hanging on to a man" back then because of a situation involving a female relative.

This extended-family member had worked to support her former high school sweetheart, by then her husband, through medical school. At about the same instant the medical-student husband became an actual doctor, he fell for someone else. He left his devastated wife and two young children in his rush to take up with the younger woman. His wife was probably in her late twenties at the time.

Somehow I became her one-person support group. I believed that I had been mandated to make the situation all better. I definitely wanted to make *her* feel better. I loved her, had looked up to her all my life, and felt totally defeated when I couldn't get her to stop crying.

When she was drinking beer, she'd pour some into a glass for me. I kept saying that one of these days her ex would be sorry about what he had done. He would realize how special she was. I suppose I did about the best I could do. Fifteen years old at the time, I berated myself for being unable to mend her broken heart. But she survived and made a new life for herself and her children.

***

The term *sexually active* wasn't used when I was growing up; at least I never heard it. In fact, the word *sex* was rarely heard. My background was so Victorian that my grandmother Mammy chided Mama, after she had children of her own, for saying someone was pregnant. It simply "wasn't said" in the company of men or children. According to Mammy, "nice people" would use the term *expecting*, but still only in the company of women.

I'm remembering Mammy being offended when someone used the word "stink," referring to fumes from cabbage cooking in her kitchen. "Nice people" didn't use that word either. Lots of taboos to remember around Mammy.

At fourteen, I woke up one morning needing a D-cup bra. At least it seemed to happen overnight. I was painfully self-conscious. No matter what the flat-chested girls thought, this was not something I felt good about. There wasn't much I could do about my big breasts except wear ugly, old-lady bras that a friend called my "over the shoulder boulder holders." The word "breast" would turn my face red with embarrassment until I reached middle age. I still can hear Mama saying,

"Hold your shoulders up" every time I was in her line of vision. Well, it felt like every time. She encouraged wearing a girdle in high school so my "fanny wouldn't jiggle." I had to be careful how I walked, Mama said, or boys might think I was easy. I only half-understood what she meant. It sounded ominous, though, so my body movements were stiff and painfully self-conscious. A massage therapist once told me that I was wearing "body armor," and it was nearly impossible to melt it. Massage and body work have been tremendously beneficial over time though, and my armor has softened a good bit.

I remember wearing a Merry Widow (Google it) under my swimsuit for water skiing. I was in high school! That was my own idea though, not wanting to look "fat." I've been less than comfortable with my body most of my life, yet I certainly wasn't "fat." I had big breasts, and probably was more "voluptuous" than other girls my age. Instead of enjoying it, I was ashamed. What a waste!

Examining pictures from my teens not long ago, I was able to see the truth of how I looked. Not only was there nothing to be embarrassed or ashamed about, I was a pretty girl with a good figure. And I never saw myself that way. Back then, the girl I saw, in my mind and in the mirror, looked nothing at all like the evidence in the photos. I still have trouble seeing what I look like when I close my eyes, and trouble describing myself when called on to do that.

There's no doubt that some of the shame so prominent in my earlier life, as well as my lessening, but still-present sexual anxiety, can be attributed to childhood trauma. I've had a knowing over the years, along with clear body memories, powerful dreams, and nightmares. Yet there have been no concrete details, visual or cognitive. I worked diligently in therapy trying to solve the mystery. I thought it might make all the difference in my life. If only I knew *who*, or explicitly *what*, maybe healing would be possible. Maybe even transformation. I wanted to know who and what had diminished what should have been my natural capacity for intimacy. Who had stolen my ability to trust?

Then, after a long, long time, I finally surrendered to not knowing. I committed to getting on with my life, even without the healing I longed for.

I know without a doubt that I was traumatized. My sense is that I was molested more than once, by two different people, at different times before I was a teenager. But I can't know with certainty. Some dream-clues led me to consider a man I'll call Seth. He was an alcoholic who did odd jobs for my mother and grandmother, usually yard work. I had suspected, vaguely, that something might have happened with him.

I asked my mother how old I would have been when he first began coming to the house. She couldn't remember exactly, but I had to be five or younger, since we were living at Mammy's. She told me that someone had cautioned her about allowing Seth to be around us children. It made my stomach clutch when she told me that.

I don't recall Seth talking to me as a child. I just remember he was around and that I'd hold my breath when I walked by him because he smelled of booze and body odor. He was poor, living on public assistance and part-time work, in and out of an alcoholic fog, no doubt struggling to survive. My mother was kind to him, especially when he became too sick to work. I remember she would drive him to the doctor and to the hospital when he needed to go. And then she'd check on him. Seth lived alone and had no family.

I was shocked when he gave me a wedding present, the caliber of gift that might have come from a close relative. In fact, I was dumbfounded, and moved, when I saw the primitive chest he had brought to my parents' house for me. It had two doors at the base and a drawer above the doors. He had refinished it. Seth told my mother it had been in his grandmother's slave cabin.

I do remember thanking him, in a proper note and in person when I saw him. Not long after that, I realized the chest could be worth some money and thought he might want to have it back, maybe sell it to an antiques dealer. He sent word that he wanted me to keep it.

Not long after his death I began having dreams and body memories pointing to something powerfully unsettling. The first dream came before I knew Seth had died. I hadn't thought about it since receiving his gift. The unnamable feeling the "something" was clearly connected to him. I remember gasping when it dawned on me. I had a visceral "knowing" that something had happened with him. I've had flashes of memory, enough to help me understand my lifelong terror of throwing up and my passionate hatred of eggs.

I began to feel physically sick when I'd look at the chest Seth had given me. What had been one of my favorite gifts now was bringing on waves of anxiety. I didn't want to sell it because I didn't want the money it would bring. It became clear that I needed to get the chest out of my house, so I gave it away.

I've come to believe that my wise subconscious has been protecting me, has kept me safe from more explicit details relating to Seth. And safe from other, more mysterious, "knowings" that come into my awareness out of the blue. All this time my subconscious, or God, my Higher Power, must have understood exactly how much raw truth I would be able to handle. I now see my "unknowing" as a kind of grace.

Despite the lingering mysteries, this is what I know today: The trauma I experienced as a child left a mark on every aspect of my physical, mental, and emotional Being. The weight of shame and my lack of self-love and self-trust are things I was able to heal, to a large extent, with Jack and with the growing self-compassion that came out of my work with him. It's a lifelong process though, and over time I've become stronger.

The inability to experience the joy and full vitality of my sexuality remains a sorrowful reality. It's the place in my psyche I have yet to heal completely. While I understand that might not be in the cards, I'm grateful for the progress I've made.

There's been a new development since I wrote this. As of a month ago, I resolved to inhabit my body more fully. You might think that sounds crazy, but I'm not alone in being someone who has sought refuge, however unintentionally, in my head. I've lived life in my mind and emotions, ignoring the body unless it got my attention with pain, or until summer rolled around, and I needed to find a swimsuit to fit it. So, toward the "task at hand" — greater body awareness and connection — I'm now working with a fitness trainer who is also a dancer. This skilled and compassionate woman has offered me hope. It's early in the quest, but I'm holding fast to my intention and working earnestly at it. While I do need to be physically stronger, more flexible and fit, those goals are secondary to *connecting with, and feeling vibrantly alive in, this body. My* body.

I wrote "The Unknowing" during the early years of therapy with Jack.

The Unknowing

In a familiar dream-forest
I stumble on a nest of tiny birds,

Stiff as communion linen.
Out of the blue, so unexpected,
My heart fell away
From the certain,
The protected and pure.

Now tears wash midnights
Clean as morning,
Soften the harsh unknowing
Of the days ahead.
The task at hand:
To find new breath & breathe it,
To find heart-truth & feed it,
To answer the crow's call
& re-enter the forest.

***

Sexcetera

Sex and the City was therapeutic for me when I watched it in re-runs. I admired Miranda, couldn't relate as much to self-absorbed Carrie; I probably identified most with Charlotte (played by South Carolinian Kristin Davis) and occasionally envied Samantha, even though she scared me a little. It was fascinating to see how the characters' attitudes about sex were reflected in their lives. It also was a little unsettling to realize that even the proper, and often naive, Charlotte was sometimes less inhibited than I.

Thankfully, I'm no longer too inhibited to talk about sex with friends. For instance, Margo, a transplanted New Yorker, told me about finding a treasure on her way home from work. She was late leaving her Manhattan office that evening, and too weary to deal with the subway, she had taken a cab. Paying the driver, she almost stepped on a beautifully-wrapped package on the floorboard. She opened it when she got home.

"What do you think was in there?" she asked. I couldn't imagine. "Dildos. Not one, but *two* dildos!" Once we stopped laughing I asked,

"Did you ever use them?" "Of course," she said, "they were state of the art!"

On the subject of personal pleasuring, my friend Marisa offered some insights from the health and beauty realm. She talks with a lot of women; actually she *listens* to a lot of women.

Marisa says that, more often than not, women are clueless about sex toys—where to find them and how to use them. So, she decided to perform a community service: She hosted an evening series on self-care, featuring sessions on fitness, nutrition, stress management and self-pleasure. There was a relaxed lecture, lively discussion, and resources for continuing education. Nothing experiential. Most of these women, married and single, were professionals in law, health care, communications, and education. Some wives, some mothers. And they were curious and shy as Miss Emily Dickenson might have been. Marisa reported that enthusiasm and gratitude were in the air, like magical fairy dust, by the time the evening ended. Everyone was walking a little taller on the way out.

***

In the city where I spent most of my adult life, there was an area populated with strip clubs, massage parlors, and adult book stores. I didn't especially like driving through there, much less consider visiting what I imagined were porn-filled, cootie-infested shops. I always associated those stores with sleaze, and in some cases I was probably right.

Although I'm eminently unqualified to teach sex education, I have a couple of shopping ideas to pass along. If you're in the market for an adult toy and don't relish going into a sex shop somewhere near you, here's an idea from my friend Lee: Take a look at catalogs featuring items for health and well-being. Those publications usually have an assortment of what she calls dual-purpose products. She pointed out that some of the massagers they offer could enhance sexual experiences with a partner or solo.

Also, I took notes when two friends shared internet shopping experiences. Alison felt comfortable at Babeland because that business is owned by women. She found shopping there was easy. (Alison is more a Miranda than a Charlotte, far more conservative Samantha.)

Then Marnie told me about Tantusinc. She appreciated that they're a green manufacturer, using processes that are healthy for the earth. They offer sex toys as well as erotic books and films, and Marnie said they're discreet. Her experience there was educational, although I doubt she will get course credit for her research.

Erotica for women and the art of self-pleasure aren't subjects of everyday conversation, not in my corner of the world, at any rate. So, maybe the health and wellness catalogs and web sites will be useful to some readers.

I've read that hard porn is a turnoff for most women, including me, while it works for most men. We women tend to like our erotica subtle and artfully presented.

As much progress as the sexes have made toward understanding one another, it's still a long way from Mars to Venus. While we're waiting for the Martians to catch up, or for someone from Venus to show up, let's agree to celebrate our fine, sensuous selves and invite more pleasure of all sorts into our lives.

Night Garden

From this night garden I call to you
Beyond lush leathery Rhododendron
Tall in its proud, watchful row,
Blossoms so bold
Their delicacy goes undetected.
In this sultry evening on Earth
I invite your senses to follow me
through moonflower vines
into the dark bosom
hiding the heart of night,

Where honeysuckle wraps itself
around tree-legs
and Lilac perfume marks a path
through Star Jasmine
Sweet Alyssum
and Four O'clocks ... come!

You think I am the Ice Rose,
Look again, deeper.

I remove mask and mantle
with soft summer fingers
unseen, unhurried
knowing the simple strength of truth,
the wisdom in slow Awakenings.

Moonlight and pulsing stars
seem at home here
where the Big Dipper
once spilled over,
seeding this sacred place.

Moon Goddess finds new places
to touch with her tenderness
here in this garden of night
of memory
of Now.

~First appeared in *AveNews*.

Part V

Plenty of Fish -
Some Men I've Known

Has not every loving mother said, "There are plenty of fish in the sea?"

For a lifetime I have yearned for an unknown *something* in relationships with men I've loved. I've wanted to be visible, known, and valued for who I am, as I am. Loved and cherished by someone who would allow me to cherish him, as well.

That hasn't happened. Rather, it hasn't happened with anyone who's available, either emotionally, legally, or whatever other reason. It could have something to do with fear of intimacy, mine and theirs.

Fantasy

Sometimes I'm
consumed
with excitement,
sometimes with fear,
at the thought
you might appear
on my doorstep,
and whisk me away
to Paris
or Bali
or the Days Inn
across town
on your lunch break,
with soggy sandwiches
in a brown bag.

~First published in *The Petigru Review*, 2008

***

Once upon a time, for too short a time, there was a man who loved me. He also loved his wife, the woman he had loved for many years. I respected her and their marriage, so our friendship would remain platonic. I knew he couldn't live with the deceit and guilt of an affair, couldn't betray her trust, any more than I could. He once confided to a close friend that he worried about me, was afraid I might be lonely. I probably was.

When I walked into a room, his eyes would dance a happy dance; his usually intense expression relaxed into a welcoming smile. Paul would say, "You are so very dear to me." Coming from him, that meant more than "I love you" would mean coming from any other man. I knew he valued me just as I was. He encouraged my writing, had written several books himself. He was impressive in discussions with other intellectuals. It was a wonderful thing to be appreciated and affirmed by him. He was precious to me and will remain in my heart. Always.

I'll never know how I made it through his memorial service.

***

I have always been monogamous, even in platonic situations. It's just the way it's been, or maybe the way *I've* been. It keeps things honest and simple, if not easy.

The first couple of years after the second divorce there was no man in my life. But the third year was different. Maybe it was because it was on a limited basis, or maybe because we trusted one another in an environment where trust is a high-risk commodity. When we became friends, he told me his wife was involved in an affair. He planned to win custody of the children. He was a good-looking man with a voice that could melt butter in an ice storm.

Peter was campaigning that year for a position elected by the General Assembly, and our friendship grew during the months he was at the State House meeting with legislators. He essentially headquartered in my senator's office, and mine, almost daily. Some evenings the two of us went dancing with a group of legislators, staff, and lobbyists. Sometimes out to dinner. But we were happiest when we could have some relaxed time, just the two of us, over a takeout meal at my apartment.

Our relationship was maddening at times, partly because I hadn't begun to heal my co-dependency. So, I tolerated more disappointment and uncertainty than I would put up with today. The timing had to be just right for his divorce to turn out the way he wanted. We never talked details. We never talked about a future together, unless you'd count an occasional slip on his part when he would casually paint me into a scene from his future. I was ambivalent, at best, about the idea of making a life with him. He said he loved me; I wanted that to be true. Usually I believed it was. But things would be different if we were married, and I didn't want that.

Peter got the job he wanted and, ironically, his new responsibilities made seeing each other more difficult. Time became an increasingly precious commodity in his life. It always had been in mine. We gradually gave up on getting together, but it was good talking with him when he called.

I reached out to Peter when Neal decided to move back to Texas and experience his last year of high school there. I was devastated and thought Peter, my close friend, would give me comfort. Even though several months had passed since we had seen each other, I was about to learn that I had stronger feelings for him than I realized.

He arrived at my door the next night during a heavy downpour. I still remember the rain pounding hard, in sync my heartbeat, when his car pulled into the driveway. The minute I saw him, I burst into tears, relief, I suppose, anticipating his support. He had never seen me cry.

The comfort he offered within two minutes of walking through the door? "If you would accept Jesus Christ as your personal savior, he would take away your hurt."

Who *was* this stranger? Speechless, I was thinking *there is no shelter in him. None.* I opened the door for him to go. When he began to speak, I held up my hand like a school crossing guard, and he stopped. Only when his taillights were out of sight did I realize how angry I was. Angry for trusting him emotionally, and painfully disappointed. I had needed a compassionate friend, not an evangelist. There was no shelter.

Last I heard he is married, his children grown. He's now a wealthy Republican. It's just as well things worked out the way they did, for many reasons. I wouldn't settle for a relationship that doesn't include mutual emotional support. And I wouldn't marry a Republican. Not even if that Republican could melt butter in an ice storm.

***

Other Fish

The Gentleman:
would have no part
of my opening doors
or lighting my own cigarette,

walking always on the outside,
taking my arm at street crossings,
politely refined
in the four-poster
of some long-dead relative.
Once he came when I wasn't there,
and planted seeds
deep in the fertile ground
at my doorstep.

The flowers far
outlived our interest
in one another.

The Miser:
visited often, drinking my Scotch
and complaining about the quality,
Rarely reservations for shared
dining experiences, except
once, a Valentine's surprise,
the waiter at a Steak & Ale
making sparks across the carpet
to bring hot bread and more water,
no re-order on wine
by the glass; his coupon wouldn't
cover it. As we were leaving
I heard coins clink on the table.
I'd bet my house he left only
nickels and dimes.
It was the last time.

The Dear One:
always had something going,
like going to the zoo, building
snow people with funny parts,
& getting stoned before
"The Rocky Horror Picture Show."
We once played twilight

hide and seek in a graveyard,
inventing lives for the people there,
holding hands on the dark walk home.
He painted my portrait once,
played songs I most wanted to hear
on his grand piano,
indulging my taste for beer
when he'd rather have Dr. Pepper.
I loved, he loved in a special way
And of course he was gay.

The Con Artist:
kept me guessing, not whether
he was lying, but why.
Truth mattered less than beauty then.
It was bad-good-good-bad,
no future I wanted to share.
He finally married someone
to get him out of debt
and wash his underwear.
He called on his wedding day
to say he still loved me.

***

I met Rex through my work at the Senate, had seen him from time to time on social occasions. He was a widower, nearly my mother's age, and I wasn't attracted to him in the least. Nevertheless, he was always gracious and charming when he squired me around to lovely restaurants and the club where he was the proud president. Even though a gardener took care of his own lawn and gardens, Rex planted a bed of spring flowers at my house one Saturday, just out of the blue. Surprised me. He was thoughtful, bringing gifts and sending clever cards from time to time. Apparently I showed more interest in his health than I realized because he began calling me "Florence," as in Nightingale. And sometime I was "Sweets." I don't think anyone else ever came up with a pet name. I grew fond of him in spite of myself.

Rex was proud of his standing in the community—both social and corporate communities—and all the status symbols that were part of his life. He wasn't tacky enough to flaunt it, though. His pride was more subtle. Wealth and "social standing" mean nothing to me. In fact, I liked him *despite* his status. In my eyes, the person who took my coat at the club where Rex presided was worthy as he.

Social skills are as natural to me as blinking and breathing. By social skills, I mean considering other people's feelings. Basic good manners combined with the Golden Rule pretty much cover any situation. So, I was comfortable in Rex's high-end corner of the world. But it wasn't where I lived or wanted to live. I was unwilling to sacrifice my authenticity to hold on to Rex's affection. I admired the kind, bright, and decent human being he was, not his social and financial prominence. He needed someone to be in awe, maybe fawn a little. I wasn't that someone.

Here's an example of something that amused me (rather than making me uncomfortable as it might have, say, a year earlier): We were out for dinner with another couple, and our server was taking cocktail orders. Rex asked what I'd like, and I said a beer. He half-laughed and said in his booming voice, "Oh, you don't really want a beer, Florence, what will you have?" I repeated that I would enjoy a beer.

I realized at that moment he was embarrassed I hadn't ordered a cocktail or wine. I imagine he considered beer too pedestrian for such a fine restaurant. The other man in our party interceded saying, "Beer sounds good to me; I'll have the same." Hard to resist jumping up to hug him. Also, it took great restraint not to say, "Make mine a Bud in a can, please; I won't need a glass."

I decided Rex would have to do his status shtick with someone else. He needed a woman who wanted to be his wife. And he found her. While we were dating, I wrote this poem:

High Rider at Sundown

High rider of the tall horse
You thunder down the valley
Outpacing the wind,
On your way to wherever
Engagement calendar dictates.

In the middle of sundown

You hurry, hurry,
Eyes and jawbone set,
Missing the fiesta of Hibiscus
Nodding as you pass.

In the middle of sundown
Your arrival is captured
By clinking crystal
Broad fingers, big smile,
The lights of your charm
Filling the room.

A small flowering plant
For the hostess
Who gives you her arm
And adoration, showing
You off like a gift from Santa.
She looks up into your eyes
As you raise your glass high
Above little conversations.

When the acceptable hour
Arrives to pack in the charm,
You go home in the dark
To set the alarm,
Rendezvous with bromide
and sleeping pill.

Luminous clock dial
Mocks the price you pay
For traveling so fast and blind
Through the middle of sundown.

***

For seven years, in the hours I wasn't working at my Senate job, I was totally immersed in the nonprofit organization I founded, no time for activities that weren't related to health advocacy or fundraising. When I met Bill, it had been "a long time between drinks" so to speak, all work and no play. Bill was handsome, a dark and brooding fellow, with a smile slow in coming, but, like the sun on a dark day, dazzling when it appeared.

We shared a liberal political perspective and enjoyed the same music. We shared some favorite movies, good food, good wine, and good restaurants. We met at a coffee house concert, both of us arriving early to get a good general-admissions seat. We were the first people there.

Little did I know I was about to become involved with yet another man with absolutely no capacity for intimacy. Bill was so emotionally walled-off that it sometimes was torturous to be with him. He told me someone in his life had said he was "emotionally constipated." He said it proudly, as if that were an honor, as if he should get an award. Once he mentioned that whatever day it was would have been his wedding anniversary, so I asked how many years he was married. He seemed shocked by my question, saying, "That's personal." He wasn't kidding. Amazed, I couldn't resist saying that it actually was a matter of public record; however, I wasn't interested enough to check. Here's a poem I wrote a few months into the relationship:

Rootbound

We're a Woody Allen movie
you and I,
neurotic to the core.
Anxious even in sleep,
you dream of going to jail
while I endure surgery
without anesthesia.
Yet there are times
of absolute comfort
despite our foolishness--
a full moon lights the ocean,
hand reaches for hand ...

We forget fear and
illusions of control,
allow ourselves to be
exactly where we are
in the moment
for the moment.
We were in that sweet space
the sweltering day
you tucked tomato plants
into a patch of dirt
in my back yard,
digging deeply
to protect tender roots.
Soon, you said, we would need
stakes and twine for support.
The plants grow taller,
roots spreading
in new directions,
stretching, greening
heaving, I suppose,
sighs of relief
at being free
from their rootbound
reality—
unlike us,
willing to trust
a deeper darkness.
We tend the plants with care
day by day,
need by need
anticipating
the gifts they will bring
later this summer.
Blossoming now,
they have a fair chance
or surviving
even thriving
in the newfound patch

of ground
that's becoming home.
I wonder if they know
they are our teachers.

***

Bill wanted me around when he wanted me around. He never said, "go away," but it was obvious he'd like me to disappear sometimes. A disappearing act was hard to pull off once there was a six-hour drive between us. He often traveled during the week, and I had just begun my early retirement. Given that, he had a reasonable argument for why I should do most of the driving and come to him. Nevertheless, it was a major effort to get there on a hellish interstate and be greeted, sometimes, by his shutting me out.

I'm pretty good at "making lemonade" so I created a travel ritual, elevating the journey to a romantic, quasi-spiritual experience. I would bring along art in the form of a rectangular wooden block with lovers embracing; that image, a collage, was on one side and an African saying on the other: *On the road to one's beloved there are no hills.* My romanticizing generally lasted until the first 18-wheeler nearly ran me off the road or an accident turned I-95 into a parking lot. It wasn't always *sweet* lemonade, but God knows I tried.

To anyone seeing us drive by in his convertible, we probably looked like a happy, carefree pair. These days, when I slip into a low state of consciousness and envy couples I see, I think of how Bill and I must have looked to the world. And the envy vanishes instantly.

When Bill had surgery for a kidney stone, I drove up to care for him on his first day home from the hospital. After several days, when his pain was gone, I initiated a talk. I don't recall the exact conversation, but I needed to let him know about the frustration and relationship grief I was experiencing. It was a "blood out of a turnip" effort, impossible to get him to show a scintilla of interest in what I was saying.

In desperation I finally said, "Bill, I have an *emotional* kidney stone, and I don't have a morphine pump." I could tell he thought I had said something clever, but instead of laughing, he actually responded to the tears in my eyes. He wrapped his arms around me for maybe a full ten seconds. That demonstration of warmth was so unusual it is indelibly stamped in my memory. We were standing in his kitchen that early spring morning, both of us in our bathrobes, our coffee getting cold.

Emotionally, it was a lot of work to be with him, and it wore me down. I cared for him, at times felt love for him. Hard work, stress, and pain are more than I'm willing to pay, ever again, for "being in a relationship." I learned a lot about myself, and I grew stronger dealing with the challenges he presented. But I choose not to learn my lessons that way now.

We said our goodbyes on the phone when we got to the end of our relationship rope. We were honest, said nothing unkind. I felt some peace when it was officially over, and some sadness. A gully-washing cry surprised me later that night.

That was only a few months before I moved from Columbia to the South Carolina Lowcountry. Bill had planned to help me move. I had worked hard during his two moves, probably financed a cruise for my chiropractor. Maybe for his entire family.

I believe Bill would have kept his commitment, but by that time I had decided his help wouldn't be worth the stress. I'm sure he was relieved when I let him off the hook. I wish him well, but I don't wish I were with him.

Jumping Rope

one
two
three
four
he's not here anymore.
five
six
seven
eight
it never really was so great.

***

"In this world there are but two tragedies. One is not to get your heart's desire; the other is to get it." I've seen variations on these words attributed to Socrates, Plato, and Oscar Wilde.

In terms of men and relationships, it's been pointed out that I'm particular. Well, yeah. Would you have settled for the men I've dated?

Perhaps the most unusual connection, or non-connection, depending on how you look at it, is a man I'll call Marco. We met at a meditation group. Yes, he's attractive, but that wasn't the compelling reason for my interest. Even though he was an intimidating force to some people, I felt totally comfortable with him from the minute we met. The attraction was simple as that. And later there was an unspoken *you don't scare me ... ha ha ha ha ha* aspect.

Another intellectual. Single, straight, and, once again, someone who shared my political views and aesthetic sensibilities. We both wrote poems, sometimes shared them. Spiritually, we were pretty much on the same page, too.

At one point I thought I was in love. I still care about him, but a romantic relationship with Marco is no longer something I would want. And that's a good thing, because brief affairs have seemed a better fit for his comfort level. Apparently unavailable men are a better fit for mine.

Sometimes I'd tell myself that ours could be a great partnership. He loves his home as I love mine. He seemed to need solitude as much as I do; he has been on his own for probably as long as I have. So, I could imagine the two of us nurturing a friendship that might evolve into something more. I imagined keeping our respective homes and independent interests. We could spend time visiting at his home and mine, each have our own solitary time and enjoy sharing special occasions, too.

I thought it would be nice "being there" for one another. We might even heal the wounds of childhood once our trust was strong enough to allow that degree of intimacy. Okay, that's a tall order. But at least we could count on each other for a ride to the colonoscopy.

Even in fantasy it was challenging. He's laser sharp and intense, ever eager for impassioned debate. I'm quick with humor and comebacks, but I'm not interested in debating him, or anyone. I'm interested in sharing intimacy through regular conversation, sometimes deep, sometimes mundane.

At one point, therapist Jack helped me see that pursuing a "romantic" relationship with Marco would be like hitting my toes with a hammer. If my fantasies became reality, it probably would have enriched Marco's life experience and diminished my own. I'd be deferring to his needs more often than not, cheerleading his accomplishments rather than focusing on my own creativity. It's an old habit, dormant for a while, but it wasn't gone. Even with the healing I've experienced, it would be easy to default to ignoring my own needs while attending to his.

These days we share a poem now and then or an e-mail, but that's about as far as it goes. Not all that different for him. What's vastly different for me is the way I see him and how I receive attention from him now. When we get together on rare occasions, it's enjoyable. I consider him a friend, if not a close one. Amazing how things can change in only a decade. There's little doubt he's sincere in his declared "admiration" and "respect." Words that were hurtful at one time describe exactly what I want from him at this point. But I admit to having wished it would work out—for a long time. *If wishes were horses ....*

Here's a poem I wrote a decade ago. As you can see, I was on the "high hopes roller coaster," headed for the zenith. My poems are a pretty reliable yardstick for measuring my growth toward wisdom. This one reminds me it's good living as a grownup again!

Beatles Rewrite

Someday you'll know I was the one ...
A forgotten Beatles song
brings on unexpected tears.

Someday you'll know: prediction
traveling fast & deep
into solar plexus,
storehouse of pain & promises
broken like wishbones
at the Sunday tables
of childhood.

Someday you'll know I was the one ...
I have known, for how long now,
that you are the one, you

off in search of Aphrodite
and tripping over Venus
at your doorstep.

Someday you'll know I am the one ...

One change in the lyric line
and I'm hopeful once again.

You will come with soft eyes,
eager for the unknown aspects,
opening to the mystery.
I will pour new Beaujolais
into Waterford
worthy of the occasion
when finally you know
I am the one.

As we make a toast
the dog will bark,
the phone will ring,
and we will hold
our glasses
with conviction
drinking to happiness,
wondering when
the fear will be gone.

I am the one.
Someday
you will know.

***

I was enjoying some newfound clarity and all the creative energy "getting clear" had released: *There will be no man in my day-to-day future.*

Then Fate, the supreme jester, tested my allegiance to that freeing, crystal-clear decision. Just last week a bright, down-to-earth, radically liberal, handsome, immensely talented man looked into my eyes, deeply, and asked for a kiss. I had no clue that such a moment would present itself. Not when we were introduced, not later at the party, not during the pitch-black, midnight beach walk three kindred spirits shared later. Not when we headed back to our friend's home to talk "for a bit." It just felt very good, real, and comfortable from the introduction forward. But attraction? It hadn't registered with me at the time.

He's not in the habit of asking women for kisses. I felt an immediate sense of connection. There was only the tender kiss and his weary but wide-awake head in my lap while the three of us talked into the morning hours, three-something to be almost exact. There were some long looks into the windows of my soul, and his. Neither of us flinched or tried to deflect the other's gaze. Ordinarily, I would have reacted with humor to ease the stress of such sudden intimacy. But there was nothing ordinary about this situation. Nothing ordinary about this man.

I learned, from the close friend who was with us, my friend since childhood and his friend for two decades, that he had some good things to say the next day. She said he continued to ask about me later. It felt wonderful knowing that; then I was a little wistful for a day or two. But I didn't turn the situation into an opera as I might have at one time. It simply was what it was. I would be unwilling to disturb my precious peace or play a part in disrupting his complicated life. I feel certain he wouldn't want that either.

It was a sweet interlude and now a memory, tucked into a warm corner of my heart. I believe we are connected and will somehow remain so. Not in a traditional sense or even a romantic one in the larger scheme of things. But there is a link that feels significant, innocent, lovely, and timeless. This poem had been waiting a long time for his magic.

You are

star freckles
on the cold, dark face
of night,
wildflowers
pushing through rock,
a bird in easy feathers
flying toward the sun,

a rich patch of earth
waiting patiently
for seed.

You are
amazement in a child's eyes
as the 12th clown
springs from the tiny car,
the passionate percussion
of summer's best memory,

cool water in the desert
and the joy joy joy
of Sunday morning's
tangled bed covers.

You are
the unseen hand
leading me deeper
into the labyrinth.

You are fearless, love,
You are fearless love.
You are.

This poem first appeared in *Midlands Woman Magazine*.

Part VI

Married

"The bottom line for me on marriage is that both people should be better in them than they are alone — not just happier, but better."
~ my wise friendUrsula

Two compelling women captured my attention on the same day. I found the first in the Congregation Circular Church graveyard in Charleston, South Carolina. Her headstone said, in part: *Here rests in peace the mortal remains of Mary, late wife of Josiah Smith, who after happily exemplifying the conjugal and maternal virtues for upwards of 37 years was suddenly arrested by the hand of Death to the no small grief of her numerous Relatives and Friends on the 3rd of July 1795, in the 55th year of her age. Descended of Pious Parents, she early imbibed the true principles of Religion, became attached to the pursuits of Godliness and virtue and for many years past was a worthy and respected member of Society ....*

Later that day I heard that Mary Parr, oldest woman in the United States, had died at the age of 113. Someone said Ms. Parr had "loved her life and working for the Red Cross." When asked about her longevity, Ms. Parr would say it was because she never married and "never had to worry about the headache of men."

I thought about these two lives that seemed so different. Ms. Parr was outspoken in crediting her long life to living it as a single woman. I suspect a positive attitude tilted the scales in her favor, too.

Ms. Parr's life had been less stressful than Mrs. Smith's, I imagined, because she didn't have "the headache" of men or marriage; in fact, she lived more than twice the number of years Mary Smith did. I was fairly certain that the conjugal, maternal, and virtuous aspects of Mrs. Smith's life probably took a toll, possibly contributing to her early demise. Later, I realized I was making a foolish assumption about that. Hers wasn't a remarkably "early" end for that time in history. Mary Smith died at 55 in 1795!

Why would I speculate on the quality of Mrs. Smith's life when that's difficult to assess even with living people I know well. And of course I know nothing about Mary Smith's inner life—what gave her joy or touched her heart. So much for my personal analytical efforts.

According to the Rand Center for the Study of Aging, numerous studies covering 140 years have been devoted to determining the effects of marriage on longevity. The Rand conclusion points out, in part, that the relationship between marriage and longevity is more complex than generally believed.

I also looked at an online abstract from the Terman Life-Cycle Study initiated in 1921. Those results indicated that consistently married persons live longer than those who have experienced marital breakup.

Individuals who had not married by midlife were not at higher mortality risk compared with consistently married individuals.

Despite the research, I don't think we know exactly how or how much a married or single lifestyle contributes to living a longer or "better" life. My common sense is shouting that quality of life is not measurable. And, as one who believes quality is more important than quantity, I've seen all the research I need to see. Nevertheless, I remain curious about whether married or single women, in general, are more fulfilled. You know, happier.

At times I have wondered whether my own life might be "better" if I had married again. The only conclusion I reached was that my life would be very different. Whether marriage or a committed relationship will expand or contract one's life experience isn't something that can be known with certainty, I suppose, unless and until we're in it.

***

Savoring my she-crab soup at lunch the other day, I overheard a man at the next table insulting his wife. I felt like decking him. Instead, I took an antacid and bit my tongue.

That same day a friend whose mother recently died told me she saves her tears for the shower or the car rather than expressing her emotions openly. She said her husband has a "sensibility deficiency." By sundown I was feeling a little jaded about marriage and, truth be told, men in general. The next morning I was saved from cynicism by the grace of Bob and Nella.

I met them in connection with a one-day volunteer project; Bob and I were packing boxes. These two have been married long enough to be grandparents. On her iPad, Nella showed me photos of a cherubic seven-month old, their youngest grandson. I wanted to understand everything Nella was communicating, but it was difficult. As she struggled to be understood, I could feel goodness radiating from this woman whose body had been ruthlessly worked over by a stroke. If there is mercy here, it is that her cognitive capacities were not affected. She seems to be relating to life from her beautiful spirit rather than a now limited body.

Nella and Bob have walkie talkies for when they're not in the same room. He understood everything she said. His devotion and their love for one another were beautiful to see.

I thought about Nella and Bob for days. Something about being with them took me back to last Thanksgiving and a moment of sweet intimacy between a young cousin and her husband: Stirring a pot he was tending, he called her by a pet name I'd never heard, "Hey, Po, how 'bout tasting this soup?" The love in his voice had given me goosebumps.

Sidebar: From time to time I've wondered whether relationships involving women years older than their men will ever be commonplace as the reverse has been forever. While I was obsessing on the subject, the Universe, great teacher and tease that she is, arranged a party celebrating the marriage of a friend. I went alone, knowing only the bride, who was stunning in a sapphire dress and being gracious to their hundred-something guests between dances. I was at a table with several couples, and the talk turned to age differences in relationships. I declared, tongue-in-cheek, that I was instituting a new policy that very night: I would no longer rule out a younger man, provided he was at least five years older than my adult son.

Across the table my new pals, Rick and Reba Ann, were laughing. "If I'd had that rule, we wouldn't be together now," Reba said. I had noticed how comfortable they were with each other, how thoughtful and mutually attentive. They'd been married almost eight years; he was twenty-one years younger. Yes, indeed!

***

The Best Things About Being Married are having someone

to roll the garbage cart to the curb.

to be your surrogate car-shopper; he won't automatically be seen as "another sucker."

to sound like an idiot describing to the mechanic exactly what noise the car was making.

to co-op the contempt of your teenagers.

who will let you know, when you're out in public, there's spinach between your front teeth—if he notices next time.

to father your children—someone they actually can meet once they're born.

whose name will be your thankless child's first word after you carry him nine months, go from sick as a dog to a blimp with legs, then through twelve hours of labor.

who's frozen with fear, just like you, when there's a strange noise late in the night; someone who's as scared as you are of the big, ugly spider, but his pride is stronger than his fear, so he takes it out. No, he doesn't kill it. He takes it outside because you want it to be outside.

to drive you home from a party. Unless, of course, he needs a ride home.

to take care of things when you're loopy after the colonoscopy. He'd better come through on this one.

to haul the Christmas tree home, banishing most of your fear that it will fall out of the trunk.

who will de-ice the sidewalk on outrageously cold mornings.

who can reach the top shelf or stand on the tall ladder that gives you vertigo.

who will say you look "great" or at least "fine" in an outfit that adds ten pounds.

who needs no batteries for handy sex.

who can find the itch between your shoulders, and other important places, in a split second.

who gives you the right to begin sentences with "My husband ..." or "My wife."

who gives you reason to buy the big pork loin instead of one chop.

who calls you a pet name in public.

who takes on some of life's burdens and a little of the blame.

who gives you the incentive to make dinners involving more than three ingredients.

who can do the heavy lifting and schlep the luggage.

But the very best thing about being married is having a wonderful someone who loves you.

And sometimes, as my friend Bev says, you just need someone around to open a jar.

***

Thoughts on Marriage

When we are young, we're blissful in the belief that love really is all we need—love and the intertwining of our life with the object of our love-lust. For youthful unions, courage isn't always an ingredient in the prenuptial mix.

But later in life, especially in second or subsequent marriages, emotional courage is what we need most. With each passing year, life grows more complex. It's layered with questions to consider before entering into an emotional and legal commitment to another.

By mid-life we're driven more by who we are and what we want in life than by hormones or love songs. By now there often are children, careers, financial complications, pets, stronger lifestyle preferences, passionate opinions, commitments and clear values. In other words, we are no longer quite so malleable. Although we continue to grow, at a certain point in life our compass is pretty much set; we've identified our North Star. As more mature, self-actualized beings, we aren't as likely to be seduced into taking a different direction. So, I think it takes commendable courage to risk losing one's compass, to risk the possibility of deferring significant goals or watering down one's own passions in favor of supporting a partner's.

My friend Ursula said something that bears repeating:

The bottom line for me on relationships and marriage is that both people should be better in them than they are alone—not just happier but better. Being in partnership should help you explore different aspects of your self in a safe place; a partner should give you peace, comfort, support, and confidence to do and be more than you would without that partner.

My own life as a married woman is like a dream not quite remembered or a painting left outdoors and faded by the sun. Today I experience marriage flashbacks with a curious sense of detachment. At times I'm able to remember some good aspects of the marriage, of being a family. The intense emotion that once accompanied the memories, both bad and good, is gone. In the early years after divorce, if someone had told me I'd feel this way now? Probably I would have been angry. I definitely wouldn't have believed them.

***

Voices from a Longtime Marriage

He:

I always knew, down deep, that I didn't want to be married to a woman I could dominate, who would allow the man to have the upper hand. Starting in high school, I'd pull away from girls I thought were meek and mild. I didn't want someone who's totally dependent.

To me, the most important thing in a marriage is that, even though you're a couple, you're still individuals. We spend time together, do things together, and each of us also has interests independent of each other. For it to work, people need to have their own emotional space ... they need to maintain and develop their own interests and their own life. You can't get married thinking that's going to end your responsibility for being an individual and developing yourself. At any given time in a marriage, I think we need to be at a point where we can still survive without the other person. Even though you can't imagine doing it and it seems like the worst thing possible ....

When the two of us talk about 'why it works' I remind her that from the first time we met, she had my admiration and respect. She said it's been the same for her.

She:

Marriage is a humbling thing, and I don't know that I'd give advice. All the things people tell you after they've been married fifty years, like not going to bed mad and all that, and I think of course I've been to bed mad. I've gone to bed in a separate bed!

For me, the critical thing is respect. The bottom line isn't about love and all the romantic notions; it's about respect being at the core. If your partner's not somebody you respect, then you can't trust them; you won't care about them forever, and you won't treat them in a way people deserve to be treated.

One of the things that humbles me about marriage, something you can't possibly tell people who are about to get married: You can't imagine how hard it can be. You just can't. It's worth it, but it's work.

I like his sense of humor, and we can laugh at ourselves. Humor helps a lot.

***

Married Again, With Children

When considering marriage, people with young children are likely to understand there will be challenges involving the children. But those entering later-life marriages don't always anticipate that adult, sometimes middle-aged "children," will be a source of stress.

Elaina is 66, feels 40. She's been married nearly nineteen years this second time. For her, the best things about a married lifestyle are *having a partner in bed, and having a travel companion, dance partner, someone to cook for, share meals and laugh with.* She, like other married women I know, enjoys feelings of greater financial security with combined retirement incomes.

Pitfalls, challenges? *Adult children have presented the most serious problems, bringing some jealousy and resentments into the situation.*

Elaina says she often does things she doesn't really want to do, like watching too much television, in the interest of the relationship. While she does pursue independent interests, she'd like to do more on her own, and she'd enjoy having more space and quiet time for herself. Her husband doesn't seem to have the capacity for deep feelings. He shows little compassion when Elaina experiences sadness, disappointment, or pain. He doesn't want to see her rare tears or hear about problems from his well-balanced and healthy wife. She has stopped wishing he were different, has accepted him as he is. These days she keeps her focus on positive aspects of the partnership. Elaina has no desire to restructure her life at this point, so she chooses to remain in the marriage. She gets support, when she needs it, from friends and a support group.

If she found herself single, would she marry again? She would not. *... maybe a live-in lover ... or, better yet, a weekend 'guest' would leave me more free time and space.*

The way I see it, marriage is like a scale. You have good and bad and you have to try to keep it balanced. There will be times when the scale tilts one way that you don't like and then, days later, it will tilt the other way, which you will love. I guess that's where 'for better or worse' comes in.

***

Ann is 52 and doesn't think of herself as 52. *I think I'm more fit now than I was at 30. Emotionally, sometimes I think it has taken me 52 years to make it to about 21.*

She's a business owner and enjoys her work for the most part, but says she's working mostly for the income. She's been in her one marriage for 27 years and has two adult children.

I asked Ann to talk about any impact the children have had on her marriage.

I think the birth of both children brought us closer together initially. As they required more time and energy, parenting was sometimes a strain on our marriage. It became harder to make time for each other. Now grown, they are once again a positive influence. They're two people we both love, and they give us a huge shared interest without the responsibility of taking care of them. I like how the kids have affected our relationship in different ways over the years.

Ann's favorite things about being married?

My favorite things have changed over time; it's certainly not the sex at this juncture, but maybe it will be again down the road. I think, for now, it's the companionship—being part of a family, a team—and having someone to share goals, responsibilities, worries, joys .... I always wanted security and stability in my life and that's exactly what my marriage has provided.

Her least favorite things?

This has changed over the years as well. Right now I would like to have a richer sex life, but I don't feel like being single would make me have a better sex life. I know too many fabulous women out there looking for the same imaginary man.

Tell me about "you" time.

I have all the time and space I need, excluding work from the picture. I also feel supported by my husband in whatever I might be exploring. In many ways I'm single because I do most of my traveling and socializing without my husband. There were years when I resented that he didn't share the same interests, but now that I've accepted our different interests it really isn't a problem. Actually, I'm happy to save his share of the travel and entertainment budget and be able to spend more time with friends.

Do you feel guilty or uncomfortable if you aren't as attentive as he would like you to be?

I don't feel guilty or uncomfortable, but I do feel a responsibility to maintain connection. For example, if I've been out three nights in a row or gone on a trip for a week, I want to spend time with him when I get home. If I've been on a vacation for a week eating at fabulous restaurants, I like to make a meal my husband will think is fabulous when I get home.

If you became single, do you think you'd marry again?

I would remarry or live with someone if the right person presented himself, but I doubt that would happen. And I think I would be perfectly happy living alone.

What "little" things do you find challenging about marriage?

Housekeeping issues—clothes on the floor, crumbs on the counter.

What "bigger" things?

Probably the biggest thing over the years has been accepting that he is the way he is and not trying to change him.

Other thoughts from Ann:

I believe women are more evolved than men at this point in human history. Women are more in touch with their feelings, empathetic to others, adept at communicating, have more complex emotional needs and desires, are better able to maintain deep intimate relationships with friends and family, are better at balancing work and home responsibilities, and have healthier sexual desires. Generally women are more capable than men at juggling all the things today's society throws at us.

I honestly think men are out of sync with the evolution of women. Sure, there are the occasional 'outliers,' but in general we're not on the same page. This explains why so few relationships stack up to what men or women desire and why they often don't last.

We wish men were on the same page; we try to pull them along, but they're just not as capable. I really don't think they are. I think we have to accept them the way they are and appreciate the areas they have evolved in. It's either that or live alone, which most of my friends seem to have done.

I never dreamed I would know so many smart, beautiful, heterosexual women, at 50 or 60, who are not in relationships with men. They have created good lives for themselves and are content to share their lives with friends and live alone. I say they are content, but actually some are not. Some of them still are looking for those evolved men that I don't think exist. Many long for a dream man. They think all the good men are taken when the reality is there aren't any 'good' men. There are just men.

Personally, I have chosen marriage. I know it might not last forever. Looking at my friends who didn't choose marriage, I feel like I have the best of both worlds. Like them, I now have the freedom that comes from fewer family responsibilities plus the security of a home base. I don't mean a house; I would have that whether I was married or not. I mean a family base. For me that's important.

***

Voices from a Longtime Marriage

He:

I think television had a huge impact on our marriage expectations—the Beaver family, 'Father Knows Best,' that kind of thing. The way the house looked, the way you behaved as a couple.

It had to be a struggle for her to put up with me because I was a real bastard. Very judgmental, rigid, hard to get to know. I didn't know how else to behave sometimes. I'd respond the way my mother used to respond to my father—blow up, insult, or get hostile. Because my wife is the person she is, she took me seriously; she also learned to adjust until she finally trained me not to be that way.

Most men I have known are extremely immature and are that until they reach a point, maybe in their 50's, when they begin to see the light. I've seen guys struggle with that. Guys will break women's hearts left and right. If a woman is patient and saw "something" in him to begin with, his good qualities will eventually percolate up. But it takes time, years sometimes. Complaints I've heard from younger women I've worked with is that their guys go out and spend most of their leisure time golfing or doing other things with their buddies. I think they're just trying to be teenagers, and they want to be teenagers most of their lives. It took me about 40 years to get through that.

If I had to say one thing to a young man today, it would be to drop all the macho behavior and just listen to the woman for a while. She'll teach you what you need to know. I think women have all the wisdom that it takes guys years to learn.

She:

My parents didn't have a good marriage. They didn't have effective communication skills, and I didn't see a lot of happiness. I think the lasting and profound effect their marriage had was giving me the determination to see that my marriage was not like theirs.

That our marriage is intact today can be attributed to our 3 C's—commitment, communication, and compromise. We always have agreed that our marriage vows were sacred; when we said 'till death do us part,' we meant that. We've had our ups and downs and, during the toughest times, the commitment aspect was especially important.

Communication was the most difficult thing to resolve because it's hard to know exactly the history someone else is bringing to anything you might say. And we have very different communication styles. He's straightforward, to the point, uses very few words. He comes from his logical brain rather than his emotions. I use a lot of words, always searching for the right one. Almost everything I say comes from my heart, and then I have to adjust it to make practical sense. So our dramatically different ways of communicating have been the biggest challenge we've had to work with.

He's generous in giving me credit, but I think we've compromised equally over the years. I have a lot of quirks and neuroses myself, and he has been very tolerant of those. He's my rock —a capable, rational person who keeps me steady. I've always felt very safe with him.

I remember saying to my mother: 'We'll be celebrating our 30th wedding anniversary next week. You and Dad said it would never last.' And she said, 'Yes, but you said it would.'

***

Sandra is a woman I got to know while shopping at a consignment store. One day I stopped by and could tell that something was afoot. Sandra was radiant. I could almost swear she was vibrating.

Lucky for me and not so lucky for the business, we were the only ones there, so we were able to talk. I knew before she said the first word that she was in love. She was, and with the best, hottest, sweetest man on the planet. He had two kids, twelve and fourteen, who lived with him. From things she said and a phone call from one of the children while I was there, it seemed obvious they were crazy about her. I was delighted about Sandra's happiness and fairly floated home on her good news. When I saw her a few weeks later, she was still glowing as she made plans for a small family wedding.

Flash forward several months: I was in her store searching for jeans that would allow for breathing, and it looked as if Sandra had been crying. She was tallying up a sale. When she was free, she told me, and I paraphrase: Prince Charming had become a toad not long after the "I do's" were exchanged. His kids had turned hostile and were undermining her at every turn. They had said they hated her. (Having had no experience with teenagers, Sandra was not familiar with the "I hate you" mantra.) She had tried everything, and she had thought they actually loved her.

And he, well, he must have been one hell of an actor. He'd been playing the Prince when in reality he was polar opposite of Sandra, with her compassionate and generous nature. The details would probably bore you or bum you, so I'll just say she has a heart to mend and a life to rebuild. The total lack of cooperation, from her man and his daughters, in her efforts toward peace, love, and understanding finally shifted in her favor. The sadness that had worn her down turned into despair, and finally became indignation.

Alone in the house one morning, Sandra gave in to an impulse to throw her toothbrush and makeup into the laundry basket. Then, she snatched her clothes from the crowded closet and "got the hell out of there." Last time I saw her, she was getting back on an even keel, still disillusioned and disappointed, but no longer devastated. Divorce in process, self-respect off life support. She regrets giving up her home to move into his, but she has a small condo near the ocean. Now she's free to walk over to the beach any time she feels like going, with no one around to spoil her fun.

When Sandra told me she was painting her kitchen floor purple, some light was back in her Irish eyes, and I knew she'd be okay.

***

Much to her surprise, my friend Isabelle remarried in her early forties and experienced the same teenager-turnaround that had blindsided Sandra. Before the marriage, Isabelle's step-daughter-to-be was her #1 fan and confidante. She enjoyed shopping, laughing, and sharing every detail of her life with Isabelle. But that was before easy-going Isabelle actually became her father's wife.

For years this girl had lived with her father, a longtime widower. I guess it didn't dawn on her, what with the excitement over a wedding, that Isabelle would be living, every day and night, in their house. And that it wouldn't be, like, a big pizza-gorging sleepover. It must have been a big adjustment for her.

Isabelle's own period of adjustment was more than challenging, and it probably was for the new husband, as well. But Isabelle's a savvy, determined woman, armed with common sense and a truckload of life skills. She loved the man she had married, even when he was hard to recognize during the first year or so. Even when her patience and compassion were worn parchment thin, she continued to care about this teenage girl who was doing everything in her power to make herself unlovable. And this princess had a lot of power. Things were shaky. Two women in a household, even when one is still a girl, rarely works out.

Isabelle's life is more peaceful now. The daughter is away at college, and the marriage is less complicated. Things are good. But it was a long, high-intensity struggle getting to "good" and dealing with challenges not everyone is able or willing to take on and work through. But Isabelle did, so we know it can be done. I credit my harmonizing Libra friend with her current "life is good" status. She's nothing short of a miracle worker. Actually, I'm pretty sure she's a goddess.

***

Married Again Without (or with Problem-Neutral) Children

Here's what my married friend Kit had to say when I asked whether she has enough time and space of her own:

'Me first' time is my specialty. I do what I want when I want. I have my own spaces—office, workout room and bedroom; I'm totally free to do whatever I choose to do. This is Kit's second marriage, going on sixteen years. She once was married for ten years, with a fifteen-year sabbatical in between. No children. Kit doesn't think of herself as sixty—more like forty.

What are her favorite things about marriage? *Having a partner I can count on; two retirement incomes, someone to house-and cat-sit when I travel. He's funny, makes me laugh.* What doesn't she like? *Having to plan around his schedule ... he's getting grumpier as he ages and watches way too much TV. That's his choice, but he's missing out on a lot in the relationship. Kit doesn't* think *she would marry again. A live-in partner, maybe. But I think a household of great women would be more fun. I enjoy doing things with women friends more than with my husband.*

I feel that we contract with our partner before incarnating, that we agreed to provide experiences that help with our conscious evolution. I try to be conscious and learn the lessons our marriage offers.

***

In a second marriage of thirteen years, Claire is 67 and feels more like 50. Both have adult children who have not presented problems. A pragmatic woman of few words, Claire says she likes the companionship of marriage and dislikes meal planning. She wouldn't want to marry again, can't see the benefits.

She says, *I think I wasted much of my youth wanting to be married and searching ... I feel for those who have never been married though. They feel left out, I think. I would advise women to take their time in getting to know the person before marrying.*

It was clear that Claire meant getting to know the person you will marry. I believe, from my own experience, it's even more important to know yourself before entering into marriage or any committed relationship.

***

Something Claire said brought up memories that led to reflection. It was about wasting much of her youth wanting to be married and searching for the right someone. I also thought about women who never marry feeling "left out." My first thought was I don't know that I'd agree with the "feeling left out" assumption. But then I thought about my friend Mary.

Mary and I were visiting at her apartment early one night, enjoying the comfortable back and forth of longtime friendship. We were fine with silence between us, too, although that didn't happen often. She hadn't felt well, had not slept much the night before, and planned to go to bed early. We parted with a hug.

The next day her brother left a message for me to call him. Somehow I "knew" immediately that Mary was no longer in this world. She had died in her sleep. It was her heart. The loss of her physical presence in my life is something I feel on a daily basis. I miss her a lot. But my point in bringing up Mary was to say this: She was a gentle and loving woman. For her friends, she was a sanctuary, a soft place to fall. Mary never married, and to be married was what she wanted most of all. She had two serious relationships, with both men abandoning her. I believe she was as kind and unconditional with them as she was with her friends. Those guys missed out on what could have been a beautiful life with her.

At times I would think Mary was idealizing marriage, entertaining a fantasy. I had wanted her to know, really know, that having a husband would not, in all likelihood, measure up to her expectations. And neither would being a wife. She wasn't missing out on as much as she imagined. Mostly, I wanted her to *have* the experience. My marriage didn't work out, but I've "been there." It's easier to be careful what we wish for once we truly understand what our wish involves.

Mary's generous heart had been broken to bits, and there was an underlying sadness about her. No bitterness. She just wanted a husband and a home with a washing machine that didn't take quarters. She wanted, with all her being, what Zorba the Greek called "the full catastrophe."

I wish she had felt complete without a man, that she'd been able to treat herself as well as she thought a husband might; to love herself as she wanted "him" to love her. She always did her best to stay positive, though. She catalogued favorite recipes, hand-copied them into books organized into categories. She was a voracious reader and a spiritual seeker. There was a feeling of deep peace in her apartment with its subtle incense and a candle always burning.

The day after her funeral service, I joined two family members and another friend to clear out what had been her home for many years. Everyone urged me to take various items, any items. "What we don't keep will end up at a thrift store," they insisted. Breaking my vow not to bring any more "stuff" into my own home, I left that day with a car crammed full of Mary's belongings. It was a sorrowful experience going through her things, impossible to believe she wouldn't need them again. Because she had honed her material possessions, and her life, to a Zen-like simplicity, I was surprised by all that remained in her closets and cupboards. A lot. All neatly arranged.

The thing that cracked my heart wide open was the number of place mats, purchased in two's, with matching napkins. The dishes, mugs, bowls. Two of each color or design. Never used. That storage closet had been Mary's "hope chest," an ark of promise.

I'm glad she didn't give up hope. I only wish some of it had been attached to goals that might have enriched her life. I believe the longing for marriage prevented her from exploring, or even seeing, some opportunities for happiness when they appeared. I wish it could have been different for her. But what do I know? None of us can see "the big picture" for another person. We're lucky if we can see some small part of our own.

***

Sally was generous in answering my questions about her marriage of more than four decades. I'm intrigued by long, happy marriages. Finding one is like seeing an exotic bird in a corn field that gets mostly crows. You just want to see it up close.

Since both my marriages involved the same man and ended each time, you might think we really tried to make it work. Or you might just as easily think that some people learn the first time around. Either way, I was fascinated by any and everything Sally was willing to share.

She's a very young sixtyish woman with a great sense of humor, a razor-sharp mind, and a Ph.D. A political activist for progressive candidates and causes, her husband pulls for the other team. When her two now-adult children were young, Sally said that ... *our roles changed to some extent, and we were worn out much of the time. But we learned to cope and conquer—sharing chores and making time for intimacy, a sex life, and time for each partner to 'own'.* Things were especially hard when one child was sick for a long time. But, she says ... *the joys of having children, and the pleasures they continue to bring, far outweighed the negative issues.*

About her marriage: *I have made it a point to retain my independence and individuality. I think marriages often fail because the man or woman (usually the woman) takes on the personality—likes and dislikes—of the other, losing one's identity in the process. When the children are young, it's crucial for each partner to claim some personal time and space and to also maintain financial independence. To be sure the wife is not in a 'subservient' position with her mate.*

I have always pursued my own interests—sometimes with my husband's wholehearted support, sometimes without. For example, he did not support my pursuit of a doctorate, financially or emotionally; neither did anyone else in my family except for two elderly aunts who always had been independent thinkers. I told my husband and family it was 'my time' and a goal I had put on the shelf until the children were on their own and until I could financially handle it.

Does she ever feel guilty when she's not as attentive to her husband as he'd like her to be? *At times I have felt guilty, but I've learned to throw guilt away. When he has needed me, I've been there.*

About whether, if Sally became single, she'd want to marry again:

I've had conversations with several of my peers on this question and, interestingly enough, we all concur. No, I don't think I would ever marry again. I wouldn't want to take the time and energy to learn to live with another person. I'm getting more and more selective about how I use my time and energy. I probably wouldn't want to make the compromises necessary for two people to share the same house. So, I also wouldn't want to have a live-in partner—at least not in my house. I would welcome him to spend the night, perhaps, but not move in. A lover would be a good thing. A man to go to dinner or the theatre and share good conversation also would be welcomed. But I wouldn't want to exchange my independence or 'freedom' for a live-in man-friend.

I've been extremely lucky to have an extraordinary relationship with the same man—who also happens to be extraordinary — for so many years. I think finding a good man is a crap shoot, and I don't want to press my luck.

***

I ask Lexy her age and what age she feels: *I'm 65 and really don't think about it very much, or about age in general. Mentally I feel pretty much the same as I've felt since, say, 25. Wish I could say the same about the physical side, but time does change some things! I feel youthful but not necessarily young. On any given day I may act 10 or 90.*

Lexy is on-call periodically at the family business where she has her own office. She's been in her current marriage for 41 years and was married in her teens for three years. There are three adult children, and about them she says ... *Sometimes they've challenged the marriage and other times they've held it together. If I had it to do over, I'd have them all again.*

Lexy appreciates *the companionship of marriage, having someone to share the joys and burdens and fun and responsibilities of life. Ironically, a spouse is often the source of those things, both good and bad.*

She doesn't like *having to consider someone else's needs, wants, feelings or opinions on a regular basis. My spouse is not overly demanding or needy, but marriage in and of itself is an obligatory state.*

Does she have enough time and "space" to call her own? *Yes, thank goodness. Oh, I suppose I wouldn't feel free to go off to study architectural ruins in Malaysia for a year, but generally I do what I want to do. My husband's responses range from resignation to acceptance to full support.*

Does she ever feel guilty/uncomfortable if she isn't as attentive to her husband as he would like her to be?

Sometimes ... and he sometimes feels the same. Neither of us hesitates to speak up if the other's schedule leaves us feeling short-changed in any way.

If Lexy became single, would she choose to marry again or have a live-in partner one day?

I don't think I would marry again, for a number of reasons. For starters, I go back to my "least favorite thing" about marriage. Between parents, marriage and motherhood, I've never had a time of not being either directly accountable to, or responsible for, someone else. It's not something I regret or resent, but I suspect I would have an appreciation for the relative autonomy of being single. Live-in partner? Likely not, for the same reason, which is not to say I wouldn't consider sharing two residences—his and hers—with someone I cared deeply about. The song 'Live Close By, Visit Often' makes a lot of sense to me. Then, at my age, estate issues become more relevant ... how best to protect and pass along assets gained in one marriage when entering another. Do-able but tricky, and it might just be easier to stay single.

I ask her about the big and small things in marriage that are difficult.

For me, it's all the same. The little things become big things. Let's face it, marriage is a lot of mental and emotional work. It's hard. Two people with two separate brains are not going to see everything in the same way or react to things in the same way, no matter how compatible they are or how long they're married. The absolute biggest challenge, in my mind, is accepting that and learning to work through, or live with, the differences in temperament, attitudes, values, interests, tastes and expectations. That it's an ongoing process only adds to the challenge ... and also can be what keeps boredom from setting in.

Marriage can be rewarding if both partners are realistic about, and forthcoming with, the give-and-take required over the long haul. Marriage's legal basis introduces a minefield of considerations. Social mores and moral/religious influences add more, and children are another whole dimension. The problem is, one can't know all that until you've lived it. It's not for everyone and shouldn't be.

Married or single, the people I know who seem the happiest and most fulfilled are those who accept responsibility for their own happiness. One can be just as lonely and unhappy married as single—and just as fulfilled single as married.

My youthful first marriage was a sham and disaster, certainly no basis for judging marriage. In the four years between divorce and remarriage I examined both myself and others, and I grew as a person. I came to understand that happiness in life, for me, is a framework of self-awareness and acceptance that includes a sense of purpose and goals. I allow my curiosity and interests free rein and find something in each day that stirs my senses or emotions in a healthy way.

When I married again, it was with a more mature view of love and commitment. There also was an awareness that it was vitally important to keep the central framework of myself—even as I learned to fit different scenarios into my life: spouse, children, family, friends, work, good times, bad times. Whether single or wed, there are always things outside ourselves that must be integrated into our lives—new 'pictures' in the framework—and the choices aren't always our own. Accommodating those is much easier when the framework of self is kept distinct and intact. And that, I would think, is true no matter what one's marital status is.

***

My friend Maria has earned a reputation for excellence at work that she loves. She's often called on to consult, not only on her home turf but around the country. Maria's career involves "assisting others in creating healthy, balanced spaces where they can thrive and be inspired." She's a lovely human, both gentle and strong, a goddess of femininity. She's also beautiful, far younger than her 61 years, and has a delicious sense of humor.

Maria answers my question about what age she thinks of herself as being:

I think that I am many ages at different times and in different circumstances. At times, I have a sense of innocence and awe which makes me feel very young and fresh to the world. Sometimes I'm weary which makes me feel older and vulnerable. Then there are times when I feel my age and realize that, along with a certain amount of wisdom and experience, I am still curious and excited to be in the world.

The mother of two adult children, she's been married more than two decades, after being in a first marriage for seventeen years. When I asked about the impact of children, she said they had a huge impact on both marriages.

It's hard to be specific here because the children were naturally woven into the fabric of our lives every day. My greatest sense of peace came when my children were soundly asleep, and I was lying next to their father, consumed by such intense love for my family that I felt completely humbled. In my second marriage, it was very challenging to mesh the new dynamics of life with a new husband and step-father. Her children were teenagers then, still feeling the loss of family life as they had known it. And their step-dad never had children.

It took lots of time and energy to hold it together. There were times I felt like leaving. Now my husband and children embrace each other in a way that is pretty amazing. He has been a different dad, but one who has been there for them through a lot of really hard times.

Maria shares her thoughts on marriage with characteristic generosity:

Perhaps my favorite thing about being in this marriage is at the end of most days when we greet each other with a hug and sit down to catch up. I think that for both of us it says: I missed you and I want to know what happened in your world. That time of checking in is important, even when it may reveal unpleasant things. It is also comforting to know that you can be yourself, and not always 'on' for everyone. Marriage can offer a sanctuary for myriad emotions and a 'safe house' for expression.

I love the way we sleep together. We fit from the very first time. My husband says it brings him great peace to be in bed with me.

I appreciate the growth that marriage has inspired. There are times when I am caught up in my own expectations so much that I fail to allow the natural evolution of relationship to unfold. Like most peak experiences of my life, they often appear out of nowhere, without using my conscious effort to make them happen. This has been one of my greatest, ongoing lessons.

My husband and I share a love of home and good food. Creating a space that nourishes us is very important. He happens to be a very good cook, for which I am eternally grateful.

I have somewhat eclectic ideas about the institution of marriage. On one hand, I feel that it was dictated by a patriarchy that simply needed a way to control and order a woman's instincts. It was also about land and power and politics. And we bought it, put a fairy tale spin on it, and proceeded to have as much power as we could wring out of it. Our normally varied and healthy sexual appetites were restricted to expression with a single human being, while men continued to roam and sample and expand their ever-widening sexual repertoire. We busied ourselves with bearing and raising offspring, buying the doctrine of submission fed to us by the reigning church fathers. Much of that suppressed energy manifested in a lot of passive-aggressive behavior that made us our own worst enemies. Many women are still trying to manipulate through submission to this day. So, in a sense, I sometimes wonder if women aren't essentially selling their souls when they say, 'I do.'

On the other hand, I wonder if it is possible that, through relationship and marriage, we are creating a completely different animal. Can it be that by honing one relationship at a time we are truly changing the world? Are we now at a point in our evolutionary process where we have the choice to take it or leave it, or make something unique and beautiful and lasting—like art, which takes us through trials and refining fires and finally arrives at that place where we stand back, admire its hard-earned beauty, and feel a sense of awe and gratitude. I have no answers, just curiosity.

What I think I know is constantly changing. I do believe that every relationship/marriage is unique, and there is no real formula for success. Mystery lies at the heart of every relationship, and we never can predict where it's going ... and should never feel guilty if it goes nowhere or ends badly. The alchemy of two individuals is never the same, and their relationship is probably best served by society's acceptance of their particular lifestyle, whether it involves children or not, exclusivity or not, until death do us part or not.

And my personal least favorite things about marriage? Sometimes I really dislike being on someone else's schedule, although I realize it is necessary sometimes, and I also expect the same. Sometimes, I feel that marriage is somewhat confining and limiting; couldn't I just zoom off to Venice and live the life of a modern-day courtesan? I am married, but not dead, after all. Sometimes, I fantasize about a temple and being the head trainer in the 'love arts' for young studs.

Sometimes, I hate checking in. Sometimes, I just want to sit at my desk and write bad poems or rant for days about whatever new soap box I'm standing on. I think I need a blog, not a new husband. I am a more spur-of-the-moment person than my husband, and that bugs me sometimes: Do we really have to do a statistical analysis of every decision? Can't some decisions be made from pure impulse?

I have always pursued interests not shared by my spouse. Most of these interests involve the spirit, and that is very personal for me. I don't really care to convert my spouse to my spiritual belief system; actually I don't have a 'system,' preferring spiritually to avoid them. But in the early years of our marriage, and after bursts of spiritual awakenings, I felt that sense of superiority that some new-agers feel, that they have to share immediately and irritatingly. My inner guru was looking for a new recruit and was sorely disappointed that my husband couldn't belly up to the enlightenment bar. So, I was disappointed and hurt that we couldn't quite connect on that level. I decided to do my thing anyway and seek out friends who could relate. It was a time of great exploration for me, and I was sad not to be sharing all of it with my mate. What was an awakening for me seemed to be totally lost on him. He was on his own path, it seemed clear. We floundered around, and at times it felt like we were coming apart. There were marital crises that took a long time to heal, but in the process, a deeper understanding and connection presented itself. I quit worrying about the state of my husband's soul and accepted that he had every right to a journey as unique as mine. And he is light years ahead of me in many ways. Of course, this is the essence of the ultimate principle of acceptance, which I failed to express. I still have my days.

Would she want to marry again if she were suddenly single?

That's a very interesting question for me. I'm fairly sure that I would not remarry or have a live-in partner. I have had sublime love and learned many lessons from marriage—and even though I still have much to learn, I think that I would not need the form that is marriage. My goal, I think, would be to cultivate my more universal feeling of love and relationship with the world at-large. Whether it would be in the realm of volunteerism, new work, or learning to more fully express love through simply being, I don't know. That is part of the mystery I embrace now.

***

Voices from a Longtime Marriage

He:

I was a young enlisted sailor, 19, when we met. She was in high school and the most beautiful girl I'd ever seen—gorgeous. High school football was a big deal, and I was with a few buddies at a game. She was with a group of girls and sitting directly in front of me; she turned around and asked very seriously, not the least bit flirtatious, 'Would you move your knees over a little so I can lean against them?'

Well, sure ... and that was the beginning of the beginning, thanks to her aching back. We were married when she was 18.

For any relationship—marriage or friendship—to work, there has to be compromise. I think you learn what's important to the other person. You learn what upsets them and you learn that, if you want the relationship to last, you're going to have to be willing to compromise. It's well known that I'm anal retentive, so I might come home in the evening and, even though she's been cleaning all day, there are things on the kitchen table. Something inside me says, 'We gotta hurry and straighten this stuff up.' But it helps to stop and remember who the other person is and how she might feel in a given situation—and then be willing to make compromises. Otherwise you'll always be in turmoil.

We're not at all alike. We weren't attracted because we have the same personalities. So my fastidious way of doing things drives her nuts, and her free-spirit approach tends to drive me nuts. But both of us have learned over the years that it's not important. So, you don't ever change who you are, but you compromise to become someone who's more accepting of the differences between you.

I can't tell you our relationship is perfect. We've had some really, really tough times. I'll be the first to admit that most of the time it was because of me. There were times she could have said, 'I'm not doing this; I'm out of here.' I would like to believe she stayed because she loves me. Her mother has been married four or five times, and her sister is working on her fifth husband. So, her life experience has said, 'If it doesn't work, try something else.' And that's what makes her different from the rest of her family. I think marriage was a commitment she intended to keep, and I believe she does love me very much. Despite all my faults she was willing to say, 'I am not walking away from this person; I'm going to make this work.'

We do argue. My younger sister came to visit after we'd been married five or six years. When she got home, she told my mother, 'They'll never stay married; they yell at each other all the time.' An outsider listening to us would think we fight constantly, but most of the yelling is in jest, part of our communication. We have really serious disagreements very infrequently.

As I've matured, I think more about our relationship. Until a few years ago, my life was mostly about making a living. It was all about the mundane, mechanical everyday things—like getting the mortgage paid, and what should we do about this or that. Now I've had some time to reflect on how much the relationship means and how important she is to me ... so when we do have one of those fights, I go to work thinking, What if that's the last time I ever see her?

Would I want those to be the last words she heard from me?

More often than not, if we have a spat about something ridiculous before I go to work, by the time I get to work I can't wait to call and say, 'I'm really sorry.' We fight and then we fight again about whose apology was better.

When I hear people say things like, 'We've been married forty years and I don't think we've ever had a fight,' I think, give me a break. If that's true, you've either got a poor memory or a poor relationship.

I think disagreeing is part of any relationship. And if two people really love and respect each other, disagreement actually can strengthen the relationship. We have fought over nothing and over some really serious things, and I think every one of those has made us closer and made me love her even more.

We started out very much in love. I think when people 'fall in love' it's more about infatuation and physical attraction. Real love doesn't just happen. You build it. I decide to love you, but we're going to have to work on this. The chemistry gets you to that point, and then it's time for some hard work.

I don't think anyone should stay in a bad relationship, especially an abusive one. But now it seems to be, 'We really like each other, let's get married.' Then with the first bump in the road it's, 'well, this isn't working; chunk it.' You're going to get divorced and remarry every time you hit a bump in the road? Both of us are stubborn, unwilling to give up during tough times. Now we need some years to enjoy this relationship we've been working on.

Sometimes I say, 'I don't think I could live with anybody else,' and she will say, 'There's not another woman on this earth who would HAVE you.' I am the first to admit I'm difficult to live with. Very difficult. So, I think I'm just the luckiest guy in the world.

She:

We talk a lot. We try every night to spend a few minutes talking about the day, not trying to resolve or accomplish anything, but talking just to share. We talk about serious things and the funny things that happen.

We make most decisions together these days—not the case when he had submarine duty for long stretches of time. I think we've always been on the same wave length and pretty much know what the other would think and expect an outcome to be. Sometimes he will say something, and I'll ask him if I had already said that; he says 'No,' yet it's exactly what I was thinking! And this isn't just from so many years of marriage. It goes back to when we started dating. It just seems like we've always been together and thought the same thoughts. I think when we got married it was a time when couples worked out their differences rather than allowing them to fester and grow. Not to say that has always been an easy path.

I think I bring out the 'lightness' in him. He has always wanted the most for me; whatever path I want to take, he encourages me to pursue it.

I think the thing that changed him more than anything was the grandchildren. He tries to joke about it, but he adores them. It's wonderful to see him with them. He's changed diapers, fed them countless bottles, and now he plays games with them. There's a special look in his eyes when he talks about them and to them. It's been a marvel to see so many levels of transformation in him, from single to married to parent to grandparent.

When he was in law school he rode the bus. One day a man approached the people at the bus stop and asked for change to ride the bus. Each said they had none because they thought he just wanted wine money. The last person in line took change from his pocket, held it out, and said, 'Take what you need.' The man took only a quarter; the generous man was blind. William said that man changed his life in a lot of ways, the most important was teaching him to trust more.

It's hard to say what makes a marriage work. We've had rough times, but we weathered them. I believe we need to work at marriage, especially in hard times. There are some things that can't be resolved and some things that shouldn't be. It's important to pick your battles; if you don't let go of some of your grievances, they can fester and then life becomes nothing but a battle.

Some things can't be explained; if you can't just leave it in your head, you might as well let it go. You can't solve everything either. If you try to solve certain things, one person will be the loser, and that is sad, or sometimes there's no understanding of what was wrong to begin with. They say not to go to bed angry, but we have done that many times. Sometimes it works best to wait until morning to get a better perspective on a situation. I don't see things as clearly when I'm tired.

I'm totally comfortable with him. It feels like I've known him forever, that I've always been in love with him. This is the time in our lives when I believe we have come full circle— from being carefree to wondering how we would make it through this or that, and back to the carefree and comfortable understanding of one another.

Two things that make our relationship work are trust and communication. I'm a very lucky person. No matter what I do, no matter what the kids do, he's always there for us.

***

Happily Married With Children, Also Very Tired

My bright and beautiful friend Leah, 42, says she thinks and feels the age she was when she graduated from college and moved into her own apartment, around twenty-two. She's married sixteen years now to the same handsome man. They have three children ten, six and two. Before the children came along, she says they were 100% a couple; now it's more like they are 99% parents and 1% couple. *We even call each other Mommy and Daddy.*

[Note to myself: Should I advise her to stop doing that? Tell her they need to get a much higher percentage of "couple" in the pie chart? I know I shouldn't butt in; she has her own journey and all that ... okay, not my business.]

She says that *the best part of being married is giving our children a strong sense of family with both a mom and a dad in the household, something neither of us had growing up.*

Leah talks about inside jokes in the marriage ... *jokes that go on for years and still make us laugh—and no one else alive knowing what we're talking about. We even have a line when someone asks us the secret of a happy marriage. Without skipping a beat, he says 'internet porn' and I say 'anti-depressants.'*

Does she have enough of her own time and space in the marriage? *She does not. Mainly due to the children, not the marriage. I do enjoy interests not shared by my husband. He's always been fine about me doing my own thing as I am about his doing his own things, too. We do read together in the same room, but never the same books.*

Does she ever feel guilty or uncomfortable if she's not as attentive as he'd like her to be? *I need sleep; usually I'd rather sleep than anything which makes me feel guilty. I hate that feeling of 'obligation.' It's hard to recapture that 'butterflies feeling' now. That takes going out on a date or a couple of days away together. It's hard to remember the couple we were before we had children.*

Any recurring challenges? *Sleeping with a snorer is very challenging. And, in addition to mothering, there's endless laundry, cooking, and cleaning. When did being married mean that I'm a maid, too? I know I wouldn't feel that if I were wealthy and had a housekeeper. So maybe that's a money issue rather than a marital one.*

Marrying again is something Leah can't imagine. *... but I've never had a problem being by myself; being alone can be nice.*

Leah says, *I've learned, after sixteen years, that being married is all about surviving the ups and downs. You have to believe that the long-term result will be worth the little annoyances as well as the larger complaints. A sense of humor helps with the smaller issues, like international travel and midnight baby-barfing; patience, tolerance, and forgiveness will get you through the tougher challenges. In general, I think not being married might create bigger problems than being married causes. Not very romantic, but that's the deal in a nutshell.*

***

At 34, Olivia thinks of herself as in her twenties, but feels thirty. She is strikingly beautiful, petite with a dazzling smile and what I consider a perfect body, even since childbirth.

She enjoys dealing in fine wines, a passion she's had for some time. Olivia likes the flexibility of her job and not being confined to a desk. She says the nature of her work is very competitive, which is not at all her nature.

Olivia and her beloved have been married for over two years now, after spending fifteen together. Their baby boy is not quite a year old. When asked about any impact he has had on their relationship, she says, *He's had a huge impact on our lives, great but stressful. Being together as a couple for so long, with only the responsibility of a dog, having a baby to care for is a big change. We love him so much and can't imagine life without him; it's the logistical aspects that can create tension and introduce shorter fuses than we're accustomed to—which can be a stressor in itself! If you're not used to arguing with your partner, literally ever, then find that the stresses of life have left you much less patient and ready to snap at each other, it can be frustrating. Dealing with the lack of sleep and coordinating schedules and household responsibilities are all stressful. Being so new to this situation, we remind ourselves that this is an adjustment period and that we still are the same people, just more stressed than before.*

In the end, the joy this child has brought is worth any of the difficulty. I feel extremely lucky to have a husband who's active in the care of our son. I can't imagine how women who don't have an active partner can do it alone.

Olivia's favorite things about marriage? *Having a best friend who's always there. In my case, someone who makes me laugh, protects me, reminds me to put things in perspective. He genuinely cares for me, and now our son, more than anyone in the world.*

As for "me" time, Olivia doesn't have much of that. Before the baby was born, she *felt free to take a class or meet up with friends.*

She doesn't think she'd want to remarry because she can't imagine feeling this way about anybody else ... *sharing the things I share with my husband or feeling as close to anyone else. I feel that our relationship is unique.*

Challenges? *Sometimes anticipating what the other person needs, things they might not verbalize. It's easy to miss things sometimes. Whether it's a big or small thing depends on whether the other person needs something like help around the house or wants some serious emotional need met.*

I asked her to share on the subject of marriage in general:

For me marriage was not a necessity, just something we finally got around to doing and wanted to do before having children. Although I still don't believe marriage is a necessity, we thought it might be easier on a child if his parents were married.

I found that being married is a little different. I think it makes us feel more like one family unit. Also, I got a little more partnership from my husband, mainly in the household, once we were married; I'm still not sure whether I'm imagining that. Otherwise, I think marriage is a personal decision, right for some and not for others, but it should be a right for everyone. It makes me sad to think that, at this time in our history, people are still having to fight for that right. If marriage is an institution that would make two people happy, who really has the right to stand in the way of that? Why would anyone want to?

I share positively about my relationship because I truly feel that way about it. I feel lucky and grateful for it every day. In fact, this sharing reminds me of all that I have to be thankful for. Not everyone has what I have, and I don't take it for granted.

***

Memo to Mothers of Growing Children

If you're married with young children, take heart from Sally. Know that you will make it through some challenging times. And you're not neurotic or self-centered; it's perfectly okay to set boundaries to get the rest you need. Staking a claim to some "you time" is important in making a marriage work and having the energy and stamina needed for parenting. There's a reason flight attendants tell adults traveling with children to secure their own oxygen masks first.

Now and then you'll need to peel the little ones off of you, give them a hug and assurances that you'll return. They will be taken care of by daddy, grandma, or the sitter. Then get yourself out in the world to recreate, or into the bathtub with the door locked and maybe some music. Maybe hire a sitter so you can take a nap. Whatever you need to revitalize.

Please don't allow guilt to creep in when you're getting your basic needs met. Otherwise? Resentments are easily built on a foundation of exhaustion.

***

At 69, Alice says she thinks of herself as about forty. She's in a marriage that has lasted 48 years, so I wanted to hear what she had to say. She and her husband have three adult children, *Good kids*, she says. There were no problems with drugs or alcohol. Her husband was away because of work most of the time, and she made most of the decisions. *My husband and I always backed decisions made by one another ... We both were very family-oriented, with church outings, vacations, and sports.*

What are her favorite things about being in her marriage?

Having a friend, lover, and companion. I feel I'm independent, but also know I can always depend on him.

Any complaints?

Never being able to fully discuss problems. He always listens to what I have to say, but rarely will there be any discussion. So, no feedback that I have greatly needed at times. I wish he would do some things on his own. In the last few years he has spent too much time with me. This has been mainly due to health problems he has experienced.

A pet peeve would be his impatience; that's a big one. And things like not hanging up his towel and not coming to dinner when he's called.

Would she marry again if she were suddenly single?

No. I don't think it would be fair to a partner, since I would constantly compare. I also know I could never love as I have in this marriage.

What else would she like to share about her marriage—the rewards, the challenges?

His health problems have been challenging. I am more than happy to take care of him when he is sick, but he has made it very difficult at times. I think the biggest challenge I've had is the silent treatment. I don't know how to deal with it, so I ignore it. I've always been treated like my spouse's 'little girl' and I don't like it. I see myself as being very independent.

I have had a wonderful life, marriage, and children. Everything hasn't been perfect, but I never expected it to be. I worry a lot, but I've learned to deal with things when they actually pose a problem rather than worrying even before a problem arises.

***

Like Alice, Lora is 69. Does she feel it or see herself as that age? *Absolutely not. I see myself as maybe sixty.*

As a counselor who loves her work, Lora says, *With my experience and wisdom gained over time, I feel that I'm at the height of my career.*

Now married twelve years, her first marriage of nineteen years ended in divorce. She was single for ten years in between. Lora has three adult children: *The children were the best thing that came out of my first marriage. And I'm happy to say that my grown children care deeply about my second husband.*

What are her favorite things about this marriage?

Having a friend I can tell anything to, having a companion on a daily basis and, of course, a lover.

Her least favorite? *I almost said "nothing" but I guess feeling expected to do all the meals and most of the cleaning in the house. But to be honest, this is my issue because I don't ask for help often enough. I would like him to volunteer. Ha!*

What are some of the challenges?

Being understood in communication and not being judged about my feelings. Communication is hard because men really are from Mars, you know. And understanding each other's sexual needs can be challenging.

Anything she'd like to share on the subject of marriage?

The smartest thing I ever did was to experience many years of counseling after the breakup of my marriage. It helped me to work on my own issues and learn healthy boundaries in relationships. I'm also glad that I waited ten years to remarry. I was told early on by a colleague that it would take ten years to meet 'a good man' and she was right. My adult children have told me how much they appreciated my waiting so long to remarry.

***

Kat says it surprises her when she thinks seriously about her age. At 71 she feels *more like 45-55, depending on my aches and pains.*

After a career as a college professor, she's retired. That doesn't mean she has stopped working; she's always working at something. Much volunteer work and some teaching and training. At present she's writing grants, and she enjoys reading the research studies. *I realize my work could provide help to a group that needs it.*

Kat found a great love at 65, and has been in her current marriage for five and a half years. She was married before, for 27 years. About that marriage she says, *I delayed leaving a miserable and abusive marriage because I worried that I couldn't provide comfortably for my daughter. I see now that, in all probability, I could have created a healthier environment alone than married. I deeply regret that I could not see things more clearly at the time. I might have saved my daughter and me from years of unhappiness.*

I'm very happily married now. We laugh together, love together, worry together, and are committed to one another's happiness. This is a very strong marriage. Too bad I didn't find my husband many years earlier. She sometimes refers to him as "the boyfriend." [Note: Kat's happy second marriage is the outcome of a positive internet dating experience.]

As for "Kat time" and freedom to pursue her own interests: *I've explored a number of new pursuits with encouragement from my spouse. I feel free to enjoy interests that are within our economic limits. I keep up with my friends, my volunteer work, employment and personal interests. We also make time to be together and share good times, but we are able to comfortably engage in our individual interests.*

What things, large and small, does she find challenging in the marriage?

Having patience with a differing view or reaction—maybe I mean 'unexpected' view. Sometimes I'm surprised when we aren't in full agreement. In fact, we are compatible on so many issues, you'd think I would just accept the differences as they exist. But I'm not always patient and accepting enough.

Sometimes we have different political interpretations, although we are fairly close on many issues. We have diametrically opposed religious views, but it does not present a problem for either of us to express our views. He's more of a spender, and I'm a saver. If money weren't tight, that wouldn't be a problem.

I'm aware, almost daily, of my great fortune in having a good and loving companion, especially in my senior years when taking care of each other has even greater meaning. We look out for one another's well-being. We share advice on health issues, and we are "watchful" of indicators in each other of unhappiness or not feeling well. That's a special gift so late in life.

Would she consider marrying again if she were single? *No more. This is such a good marriage; if something happened to separate us, I would want to be content with memories of something very good found late in life and valued immensely*

Part VII

Single

It would take a very special man to take
the place of no man at all.
~ Anonymous

My friend Karla is an intensely focused executive, vegetarian, and rescuer of animals. She was once married for a short time, has been divorced for years now. She works hard at her career and stays in shape, exercises religiously. She's forty-five, and you'd guess thirty-something. China-doll skin, raven hair, bright blue eyes and of course a totally-fit body. I see Karla as independent and fearless in many ways. Yet the thought of being without a man seems to scare her.

She's had a couple of enduring relationships and recently an unfortunate one. Down deep, she still believes it could work out "if only ...." Brian has been gone for nearly a year now.

What Karla wants to have with a man, and what she relentlessly pursues, is an intimate relationship with deep communication—even about the minutia of day-to-day living.

I have friends, loving couples with good communications between them; they seldom share the minutia. TV's Dr. Phil McGraw thinks that, for talking about certain things—like what a friend really meant when she said something or other and whether this dress makes your butt look bigger than that skirt—women need women friends. Most guys don't want to have those conversations.

For the record, I agree with Dr. Phil. Karla doesn't. Karla doesn't have many women friends. She's been all about the man in her life. Or the man recently out of her life. Or finding the next one. She's convinced she can have the idealized relationship she envisions— moonlight, roses, and minutia. For her sake, I hope Dr. Phil and I are dead wrong.

One day I looked into Karla's red, swollen eyes and said, "You really need to make time for your women friends. They're the ones who will be there for you no matter what."

There were times I thought she'd break into a million pieces. She couldn't sleep, lived on caffeine, and her nails were chewed to the quick. Karla found a counselor to help her get over this last fellow, and she's making progress.

She couldn't stop believing their relationship would work out. If she were thinking clearly, she wouldn't want it to work out. This otherwise rational woman totally lost her senses when it came to that agonizing man. At first I was more than willing to hear about her struggles with Brian. But, after about a year of his emotionally abusive behavior, I couldn't deal with the situation any more. Karla never could see, or maybe admit, that he often was verbally and emotionally abusive.

Sometimes it's hard to step out of our own operas far enough to see what's really going on.

She might not be done with him, but I was, so I set a boundary. "Karla, I love you. I'm glad to be here for you in other ways, but when we talk about Brian I feel furious that you're not angry. I can't listen even one more time while you excuse his behavior with 'I think he might be depressed' or 'He had a sad childhood.'" It was a hard boundary to set.

If only Karla would take a relationship sabbatical long enough to be with herself for herself. If she could give her longings a rest, resist the compulsion to click on the internet dating sites—just until she reclaims some personal power—her odds would be better for having a healthy, sustainable relationship. (Says this all-knowing one with no man in her life.) I wish she could see that "relationship" has to happen with herself before it can happen with anyone else. But *if wishes were horses ....*

The Brian boundary will keep me from saying all that. She's entitled to learn her own lessons in her own way. It's her life, her pain. But it is hard to witness, even harder not to meddle. Mentally revamping other people's lives is something I get into from time to time. It's been a convenient detour around sorting out my own mess.

After a period of adjustment, Karla stopped mentioning Brian. It was the only way to preserve our friendship. Tough love is exhausting.

***

Journal entry: There's a bird on my car, a Mockingbird, fluttering his wings the way birds do when they flirt. This is the second day I've seen him. At first I think he's looking for food in the crevice around the windshield. But he goes to the side mirrors, then back to the windshield and windows. Thinking he must be looking at his own image, I name him Narcissus.

But later, I get it. He thinks his reflection is another bird. He's not giving up. It's doubtful he's left the car all day. Bless his heart, I think he's in love!

Bird update: Day 2 and he's still out there, gone crazy for love. The fluttering seems more intense, almost desperate, today. Will he ever realize he's under the spell of illusion? Poor little heart, pounding for what's destined to be, at best, a one-sided relationship.

Ever been that bird? Yeah, me, too.

***

Journal entry: Okay, I'm becoming as obsessive as the bird. Back and forth to the window, watching. Not much light left at the end of Day 3, and he's still flapping and fluttering. The pursuit has gotten more, not less, fervent. I can barely see him. Time for all sane birds to be settled in for the night.

Birdwatching has become theater. He thinks his reflection is his soul mate. But the soul mate remains untouchable, even after fluttering right back at him from mirrors and windshield. I'm feeling a little wistful now, watching this drama unfold, becoming the tragedy of unrequited love. He can't get enough of wanting her.

Lesson for girl birds: He's relentless in his pursuit, why? Because he's getting nothing from "her." Nada. Zip. Zilch.

***

Journal entry: Early morning, Day 4. I'll be moving the car today, leaving my laptop and the bird for food shopping and other errands. I'm wondering what he'll do when I drive away with the object of his desire. Would Mr. Mockingbird follow me the six miles into town? What will he do with his obsession when we're, *I'm,* gone? Before getting to the window, I laugh at my fool self. What the hell will I do with my obsession if he's not out there?

But he's still out there, going through his mating ritual, feverishly hopping from windows to mirrors to windshield. She follows him, of course.

But something's different today. Are you ready for this? Now the two-timing little shit is giving the business to the bird in the Ford Focus next door. Apparently he's not devastated that the first object of his affection never came out from behind the glass.

This fellow's not hearing violins; he's way too revved to entertain melancholy. Probably called Bird #1 a tease, cut his losses, and moved on. No doubt he enjoyed the chase.

Later, walking to my car I realize Mr. Mockingbird has given me some food for thought and covered the car with reasons for a professional wash job.

***

The Best Things About Being Single:

Having dominion over the thermostat year around.

Having absolute control of the remote. You even get to choose all the movies.

If you want to get up at 3 a.m., click on some good music and dance—or decide to shampoo the carpet—nobody complains or makes you an appointment with a mental health professional.

Nobody asks how much anything costs or gives you the evil eye if you come home with a little dent in the damn fender.

You never, ever, ever have to hear a sports announcer's voice in your home. Unless, of course, you like sports.

You can enjoy great sex and nobody expects you to rate how good it was or to cheer afterwards.

You can eat all the broccoli and baked beans you want and skip the Beano.

You can spend the entire weekend in your PJ's and no one walks around staring at you with a furrowed brow or superior smirk.

Nobody has to like your friends except you!

You don't have to tolerate anybody else's friends or business associates.

No one is at home to spoil your happy moods. Or around to deprive you of the bad ones.

You can have a pet or not have a pet. A pet can sleep in your bed if you want. Nobody else gets a vote.

You can sprawl all over the whole bed all night long, unless you have a pet in there.

Your home can be a reflection of you, as neat or untidy as you choose. You can paint something pink or lavender; there can be florals and chintz. If you like.

You can go or not go to the party. If you go, you can stay as long as you want, or slip away ten minutes after you get there. No consultation required.

You can order Chinese, go to the four-star bistro downtown, or have cold cereal any old night you choose. No drama in the decision-making.

You can have friends over, even rowdy friends, and they can stay as late as they want, even all night. If you want.

You can squeeze the toothpaste tube anywhere and use any razor that's handy. They're all yours.

You can talk to yourself, have entire conversations. I do it all the time.

You can go out late and stare at the stars and exclaim about the fullness of the moon. Or howl.

You can make holiday plans that suit you without turning them into an opera.

When traveling, you might meet interesting people if you're alone. (If you can afford the trip you can afford to pay somebody to carry the luggage.)

You can meditate, uninterrupted. All you want. Long as you want. No one asks, every time, what you are doing or where he put his glasses.

You can have a phone session with your astrologer or psychic. How much it costs is nobody's business.

All the cashews in the mixed nuts are yours.

You get to go on or off your eating program any time you want without becoming an object of ridicule.

You get to decide whether you want a man in your life. And you get to reconsider whatever decision you make whenever you like.

Nobody cares that it took three hours to get dressed or that you tried on every garment in your closet. Nobody is there to witness the obscenities as you put it all away late that night so you can get into bed. Or maybe you just crash on the couch.

No inquisition over the chocolate chip cookie disappearance. No complaints about teeth marks in the cheese.

The best thing about being single, any way you look at it: You're FREE, babeee!

***

At forty-nine, Leila s living single after being married to her high school sweetheart twenty-seven years. No children. She was divorced nearly two years ago. Even though she sometimes feels lonely as a single woman, she often felt lonely in her marriage, too.

Leila has enjoyed a career in esthetics, as both practitioner and teacher, but she hasn't been able to find work since her employer's business folded two years ago. She's making it on her divorce settlement and some unemployment for now.

She's not dating anyone or making an effort to meet men. The few times she has met someone she says, "The Universe seemed to step in and prevent the connection, maybe to save me from myself. I'm going on with my life. If a relationship comes across my path, fine; if not, fine."

She said she was told by an astrologer that she will marry again. "If that proves true, he'd better walk on water," she says. "Otherwise, it's just not worth the sacrifices to me."

Leila's two dogs bring love and companionship to her life. She treasures her freedom and having her own space. She says greater financial security would be nice, and she likes the idea of sharing life's ups and downs with someone. On the other hand, she treasures her independence and doesn't like the thought of losing it. She's still not comfortable having dinner out on her own yet, preferring to eat at home or get take-out unless she's eating out with friends.

[Note: It took a long time for me to be comfortable as a "party of one" at really good restaurants. But after a little practice, it has become something that gives me pleasure. I no longer take reading material. My intention is to enjoy the ambience and savor every pricey bite.]

What has Leila learned?

That you can't have a healthy relationship if you aren't emotionally healthy and your partner isn't emotionally healthy. You can't truly love or accept love from another if you don't love yourself. Desperation energy just pushes what you desire farther away or attracts desperation energy. Want and need are two very different things. I want to have the 'right' partner in my life, but I definitely don't need it. If it's not right, I am not interested. As for myths she can debunk: That marriage is easier than being single. Marrying means you'll have someone to take care of you. Being single is not as fulfilling as being married and having children; single people are not really happy.

After getting through a painful marital breakup and grieving the loss, Leila now is creating a satisfying life for herself. Having the freedom of her own time and space, no longer using her energy to sustain a difficult relationship, she is growing spiritually and emotionally.

I think Leila was brave to move to a state and city unknown to her, risking major change on the heels of an emotionally draining divorce. Taking chances can be especially scary when dealing with more than one significant life change. But risking big change—where we live, our life's work or our relationships—is often worth it. And if it turns out not to be, we can risk again. And again. Sometimes it's easy to get stuck in limited thinking when it comes to choices involving change.

For Leila, allowing courage to trump her fear of the unknown has paid off in a big way. *I love my new adopted city better than any place I've lived and almost more than any place I've ever been.* And after living in a small apartment for a while, there was another in-city move. *Thanks to the generosity of a friend, I was lucky enough to move into a small, completely renovated home in a highly desirable area. I could never have afforded it otherwise, and I love it!*

Next time you find yourself hesitating on the brink of a risk that feels right, maybe you'll think of Leila.

***

Marty, at sixty-one is a single woman, a social worker with one adult child and three grandchildren. I asked her to share some of the challenges in her marriage of fourteen years. She became pregnant just after marrying, and child-rearing was a challenge early on. Then, over the years she dealt with her husband's infidelity and his asking for a divorce.

Some good aspects of marriage, as she sees it, are safe sex, a "best friend" she could confide in, and more income. *I loved being married, being a family. I loved my home and haven't owned a home since I was divorced. Myths about marriage? Till death do you part; the sense of security can be unfounded.*

After grieving the loss of her marriage for a decade, she became willing to open herself to a relationship. She was in an intimate relationship for about ten years, with her partner ending it. So, dare I ask whether she would want to be married or in another committed relationship? I dared.

Not really. But, if so, it would have to be with a like-minded other, so it's not likely. Being devastated twice is enough.

The good things about being single? *Having my own space, not having to answer to anyone, and not having my attention constantly on a man. I do miss sex and other aspects of intimacy, especially the affection.*

Marty tells me about a single friend who (after two brief marriages when she was young) has celebrated her independence for a long time now. *She has a lovely home and isn't interested in living with a man. She enjoys being in her own space and entertaining her friends.*

Now that our estrogen levels are non-existent, there's no more seeking men out. My friend and I work together and enjoy the occasional good-looking man who comes into the store. We look at each other, sigh, and laugh.

Sidebar: What I'm hearing from a number of women who have navigated menopause is that their libido is very much alive and now resting, more or less, in a comfortable place. Think of a hammock under a big shade tree rather than a roller coaster. Most of the women agree it's actually a nice change. With the right stimulus, the libido becomes your amigo, more than happy to cooperate.

The difference I'm hearing from women now is that it no longer plays a major role in daily life. Although libido is a factor, I agree that it's not the driving force or the deciding factor in choosing to be in relationship with a partner, in or out of marriage. As my friend Julie said, "With a good vibrator and plenty of batteries, you're good to go until you're gone."

Of course for some women hormone levels impact libido more significantly. And, as you know, there's an abundance of conflicting, confounding information about hormone replacement therapies. Self-education on this subject is important for many reasons. It's critical in communicating, and sometimes negotiating, with health care providers. That's the only way to ensure getting our needs met. One thing I try to remember is that doctors don't have time to stay current on all the recent studies and, just as importantly, most aren't trained in the health-crucial field of nutrition. Some MD's I've met have discounted the importance of nutrition and declared nutritional supplementation useless. I feel strongly about the supplements I take and continue to use them. That's where self-education helps. After all, we are the CEO of our own health and well-being.

I also keep in mind that "lobbyists" for most doctors—and a significant source of information for them—are pharmaceutical reps promoting products linked to their own economic interests. When results of a new study are released, I check to see who funded that study and remain mindful that results can be presented in a variety of creative ways.

It's a gift to find a personal physician or family nurse practitioner who sees patients as more than the sum of their body parts, a practitioner who understands the impact of emotions, mind, and spirit in our overall state of being. [Note: If you're searching for such a practitioner, you might want to check out the American Holistic Medical Association at holisticmedicine.org. Also, a friend of mine is passionate about her professional career in educating women about the hormone connection to well-being and options available to them besides synthetic hormones. You can find information at her web site, hormonelady.com.]

Marty: *What I miss most about being in relationship with a 'significant other' is having a man who cares about me, that I can be intimate with. I miss talking ... I miss having an automatic someone to do things with, to share life with.*

My world doesn't revolve around a man or the lack of one in my life. I like being single because my attention can be on what matters most to me, my spirituality, for lack of a better word. For me that means seeking truth through reading and studying with teachers whose teachings I resonate with. I want to be at peace as much as possible. That's my goal now.

Marty sent me a handwritten note saying that my questions had led to some meaningful reflection about the relationships in her life. She said, *What I'm left with is a lot of gratitude.*

Would I change things? There is a little hesitation because of all the pain, but, no, I wouldn't change things, even though they turned out the way they did. I'm grateful to have had the experience of being married, of sharing a home and creating a life with someone, being a family. I'm also grateful to have been in a serious relationship for a decade after the marriage ended.

Although the trauma and pain of breakups tend to cloud the appreciation, I think my life has a richness and depth of experience because of these relationships.

***

Barbara is someone I admire. She's 52 and hasn't married. Although she remains open to Mr. Right, she hasn't put any aspect of her life on "hold" waiting for him to show up. Barb would like the emotional security of feeling connected and the intimacy and mutual support of marriage. She thinks it would be good to be a couple who would care for each other in old age.

Having a beautiful home matters to her, and she has worked as many as three jobs to make having the home—and other things she wants in her life—possible. Her home, she says, is *where family and friends can come and feel the love, knowing they are always welcome.*

Over the years Barb has continued her education while working high-stress jobs. She's now going for another degree. This one involves a two-hour commute every other weekend for classes that last all day Saturday and most of Sunday. And still she's working weekdays. I marvel at her energy and respect her determination; I get a kick out of her come-to-the-cabaret approach to life. I love her openness.

Although she'd be more than delighted if "He" appears, this Wonder Woman hasn't stood still waiting. Instead, she's created a fine life for herself. Like every life, hers has brought challenges, pain, and hardship; she has navigated through those times without losing her positive attitude, her zest for life, or her mojo. She enjoys her career as an educator and looks forward to a comfortable retirement down the road.

I wish you could know Barb, especially if you're losing sleep over not being married or in a committed relationship. She'd show you, without even trying, how to be more than okay with living independently and she'd make you laugh a lot in the process. She's generous with others and with Barb, treating herself regularly to *fresh flowers, wine, bubble baths and marathon shopping sprees.* She emphasizes that she buys really good wine and fine perfume. As the song says, "She works hard for the money" and she totally enjoys everything her money buys. Here's to you, Barb.

***

I was glad to hear from Monica, a friend of a good friend, who was willing to share what single life is like for her. She was warm, down-to-earth and straightforward.

Sometimes I feel my age, which is 45, but usually I think of myself as about 25. I've been married three times, no children. Single now for about eight years. My third husband was 15 years my senior and seemed more like 25 years older. We had a pretty good life together for several years in a marriage that lasted six years ... the marriage seemed all about what he wanted in life, and my small role didn't matter much. Towards the end, I felt like I was drowning.

I'm not dating anyone now, not sure how to meet people any more. The dating online thing was a waste of time for me. I live in a city where guys my age seem to be interested only in 20 or 30-year-olds. I have no problem dating older men, but I'm not sure where they hide out these days.

She's not sure she would want to get married again, but says, *I don't think I want to live alone for the rest of my life either. But it's not all bad being on my own. I can come and go as I please and not have to take care of anyone but me. I can 'lay up sorry' on the couch and watch whatever TV I want or stay in over a weekend and read, or go out every night without having to answer to anyone. I do miss the sex though. And I think sometimes it would be nice to have someone to go out with, do things with. Then again, I have a friend whose husband does nothing with her. He works a lot, doesn't seem to be involved in the workings of her life—so, who knows? Going to parties and other events are the times I wish for a partner. But I do have a couple of male friends I can invite when I decide to do that.*

My home now is a 600 sq. ft. apartment built in 1927. It's beautiful! I love my little home where I'm surrounded by all the books, art, and other meaningful objects I've collected over the years. There's a little front porch with old wicker furniture and lots of plants; I keep bird feeders filled for my feathered friends and pretty much live out there when the weather permits. There's lots of natural light in the apartment, and it feels very comfortable and cozy. Home is where my heart feels best.

I usually cook several times a week, making enough to take lunches to work. I actually learned to cook only a few years ago. I enjoy the whole process of cooking and eating—deciding what to cook, shopping for ingredients, preparing the food and eating it. I usually eat in front of TV. When I go to a nice restaurant, I sit at the bar. You can always find someone to talk to at the bar, even if it's the bartender. I wouldn't sit at a table alone or take reading material because that puts too much attention on me. Actually every place I go, people make me feel like they're glad I came.

As for career, I'm a part-time faculty member at a community college and work at another full-time job there. The teaching I love, but the other job is just for benefits. I need it until I can teach full-time or find something else I really like. I took a year off in 2007 and spent every penny I'd ever saved. I was completely broke, but I had a hell of a time, and it was the best thing I've ever done for myself.

I have a little dog named Scooter, the joy of my life. I never knew I could love so unconditionally or that I could be loved in that same way. He goes everywhere with me. My friends know if Scooter's not invited, I probably won't come. He's well behaved and a certified therapy dog, so we can visit nursing homes. Now if I could find a man I could love half as much as Scooter, he would be one lucky man!

I'd give this heads up to women about to become single: You probably can't count on your married friends to be there like they were before. They have other priorities, and you won't be one of those priorities.

As for myths about marriage, one of the biggest is that a man is going to make your life complete and fulfill you. Truth is, you have to get there on your own; no one else can do it for you.

For so many years I was afraid to be alone. I felt like I would die if I had to sit at home by myself, so, I went from one relationship to another to avoid spending time alone. I would think that if I could just find that special man, my life would be complete. If I could find the one true love who's waiting for me, all my worries would be over.

I'm here to tell you I was 37 or 38 when I realized my life was already complete. I control the happiness switch. It's all up to me.

Until you can really enjoy the life you have made for yourself, no one can possibly 'make you happy.' After you find happiness within yourself, it might be time to consider finding a partner to share it.

***

Roz, a talented artist I admire, is in her 40's, feels more like her 30's, and hasn't married. When I asked what has contributed to her remaining single, she responded without hesitation, *FREEDOM!* She's not sure she wants to marry.

How is Roz meeting men? *Luck. Mainly by being myself. The more I am into who I am, the more guys show up. But you can't be lucky all the time. And if you're the slightest bit desperate, every man in the world can tell.*

How does she feel about going out alone? *I will go alone to a nice restaurant, and I prefer to eat at the bar. I love going to gallery openings on my own. I want to experience the art; that's why I go. If I meet people there, that's a bonus. If I see some old friends, that's good, too.*

Roz advises, *Find your passion and follow it. Every time I dig really deep and focus on my life and myself, a man shows up. I think the more I am into me, the more evident it is that I'm a confident woman. And men love confidence in a woman.*

***

Independent Women Share a Saturday night concert, a solo vacation, and a holiday celebration for one

Judy and Me

There were years after the divorce when I wouldn't consider going out alone in the evening. A movie matinee, sure, and maybe volunteering to usher at the community theatre, staying for the show. But the dark of night would find me out only in the company of friends or with the occasional date.

What it took to get me over that particular fear hurdle was a Saturday morning call from my friend Pat. There might be no such thing as a free lunch, but sometimes there's a free concert ticket; she offered me one for that night. Judy Collins would be playing at the Auditorium downtown. Since Pat is married, my first hope was that maybe there were two tickets, and I could invite another friend. But her husband had no interest in hearing Judy, so she had gotten only one ticket. She encouraged me to go; it was a really good seat. Judy Collins was one of the few entertainers at that time who could make me pause before saying, "no." I had all her music and really wanted to see her, hear her, in person.

No performer's pre-show jitters could have been worse than the anxiety I felt after saying "yes." I edged right up to the brink of backing out several times. *It's so dark downtown; probably have to park blocks away ... I'll be out by myself on a Saturday night.* It's amazing how hard I was willing to work at self-sabotage.

At times I'll have a "knowing" in my solar plexus, the equivalent of a siren going off and a billboard flashing NO! DO NOT! The Judy Collins concert anxiety was not such a warning, and I knew it. This was about my fear of the unknown and the fact I'd convinced myself I couldn't see well enough to drive at night.

It was worth an afternoon of anxiety because, once I was all dressed up and on my way downtown, I was fine, and totally astonished that I was fine. I'd heard that fear and excitement are first cousins, so I invited excitement to join me that Saturday night. Fear had been my companion far too often.

Parking was not an issue, after all. There was a well-lighted parking lot right next door to the Auditorium, well worth a few bucks. Once inside, I was ushered to one of the best seats in the house: orchestra section, middle of the third row.

Well, the concert was sublime. The artist's voice so pure, the musicians in perfect form ... *Send in the Clowns* ... *Amazing Grace,* all the songs that had spun around my turntable (yes, turntable) countless times. And there were a few new ones, too. I was transported to what Heaven might be for me. Euphoria. Nirvana.

When she sang, *Bird on a Wire,* Judy and I made, and held, eye contact with the line "I have tried in my way to be free." I felt my eyes pooling with tears, and I'm pretty sure I stopped breathing.

Sometimes I still think of Judy Blue Eyes and want to tell her that I, too, was trying to be free—that going to her concert that night was the first step on my road to freedom.

***

Vacationing Solo

My friend Cynthia's had some great solo vacations. One year she and her college roommate went camping in South Dakota. That adventure turned out well, even though neither of them had ever pitched a tent or shared a primitive camp site with hungry mosquitoes.

When I asked Cynthia to refresh my memory about her trips, here's what she shared:

The trips I've taken alone have been some of the best vacations of my life—mainly because I experienced everything without the distraction of conversation or attention on another person. That sounds selfish, but it allowed me to be fully present with each experience, much more aware of all my senses. I was able to take everything in completely, with childlike wonder.

My trip to Arizona turned out to be a spiritual journey because I've never felt so much a part of nature. Even with other people around at times, my attention was focused on the beauty of nature all around me.

I got a flight to Phoenix, then rented a car and drove to the Grand Canyon. On the way there, I stopped at Arcosanti and Sedona and loved learning about Arcosanti and seeing the artisans. Sedona was magical, one of the most beautiful, spiritual places I've ever been. I had never seen such red rock. I was there at sunset and visited a magnificent chapel in the rocks; I visited mineral shops and took nature photos along the way.

As I drove up to the Grand Canyon there were fields of yellow flowers like I've never seen before or since. As I came into the park, I kept wondering, 'Where is the Canyon?' When all of a sudden there it was, I couldn't believe what I was seeing!

I stayed in a cabin in the Canyon and watched the sun rise above the rim each morning. And saw it setting each evening. I hiked with a group, then went, on my own, beyond where the group had gone. It was dusty, windy and a bit intimidating, yet beautiful.

After a couple of days there, I drove to the Painted Desert. It was monsoon season, and I saw only one or two other cars in the area. I parked the car and walked around. The sky was that beautiful color it turns when a storm is coming. Lightning began to light up the sky and, as I looked around, it was as if someone had poured bags of gemstones in the sand—all different colors. There were mounds of these gemstones everywhere; once again, I'd never seen anything like it. After seeing the Painted Desert, I went back to the Grand Canyon for a couple of days, then on to Phoenix to catch my flight home.

I've had two vacations in the San Francisco area, went by myself both times. The first trip was part of my spiritual journey, and I went to a retreat in Tiburon, just outside San Francisco. While in San Francisco, I stayed in a most charming hotel, owned by a French family. Unlike most larger hotels, it was more personal and quaint, with beautiful art all around. There was one of those old elevators and wonderful breakfasts each morning.

As I write this, what dawns on me is how much I was aware of everything around me when traveling by myself. There were only the surroundings, all new and exciting, totally mine to savor. Little things brought so much pleasure and took on so much meaning. Traveling alone has been a freeing thing for me.

As far as being in a relationship, I would love to have a soft place to fall, someone to hold me tight, love me and tell me "everything's gonna be all right." But I'd still want to take a solo vacation now and then. There's nothing like it.

***

Party for One

I can do a life review in five minutes by remembering how I ushered in specific years. The comfortably happy ones spent with close friends, laughing and clinking glasses at midnight, a bonfire and marshmallows toasting on coat hangers. Then there were the years when my frenzied commitment to fun ended up being anything but. Those generally involved a date or husband who couldn't metabolize the bubbly and needed a nanny-driver before midnight. There were the big, noisy celebrations with sloppy midnight kisses from less-than-enchanting strangers. And of course, I can't forget the New Year's Eves I hosted a pity party for myself, when my only guests were the shivering souls waiting for the countdown at Times Square. I remember all those nights more clearly than the resolutions I made and broke. Sometimes we do live and learn; I have learned not to torture myself with resolutions.

For a while the last night in December became just an ordinary night, usually marked by forgetting to soak the black-eyed peas for New Year's dinner. But last New Year's Eve was far from ordinary; in fact, it was my best ever.

I can't say what inspired me to create such a deliciously sensuous evening. But I managed to celebrate all aspects of myself by including them in my plans: Special ritual for spirit, and chocolate and sparklers for the inner child. I would indulge my mature woman taste with a special wine and dinner. A lovely bath for the body. Candles, flowers, and music to satisfy my Libra sensibilities. And for my emotions, a promise of release. All this in the comfort of my own casita.

Last New Year's Eve I was awake and keenly aware of symbolism in so many ordinary things. I lighted candles and sat in silence, watching clouds in shades of pink and orange shape shifting moment to moment. I counted five egrets flying home before the sun disappeared behind the tree line on the western side of the lake. I meditated on the shadows of cypress trees in the water—so grand, these mossy-haired goddesses. They've been around long enough to know things.

When it was too dark to see the shadows, I switched on a lamp and came out of the silence with a CD of mystical chants, my sense of peace deepening. Reflecting on the past year, I became aware of things in my life I wanted to release. Thoughts of inadequacy, time-urgency, the pain of lost friendship, the grief of death. And I made a list of those things. I sat with the list for a while, allowing tears to come and fall until they stopped. No rush. Then, with a benediction of sorts, I burned the list in the sink, then gave the ashes to Mother Earth out back, near the lake.

Next there was some seriously good cheese and uncorking the wine. Then, the nice dinner I'd made earlier, jasmine rice and shrimp. I was intentionally mindful of every delicious mouthful: spices, textures, the perfect balance of the wine. Dinner music by Andrea Bocelli. Ahhhhh, yes.

After the meal, I spent some time writing my intentions for the year before moving on to the next ritual. I ran water into a bucket, until it was half full, and mopped the kitchen floor. This is the first part of what I recall as being a South American New Year's tradition. It symbolizes washing away the old, making a clean slate. Only for a special ritual would I not complain about mopping.

After the floor cleaning I rewarded myself, a mineral bath with lavender and candles. A beautiful experience and, afterwards, no apologies for the world's softest granny gown and slippers with socks.

There was dancing to some high-energy African drumming and New Year's wishes on the phone with friends. Another glass of wine, with Keb Mo singing his blues, then dancing to Joe Cocker, *Unchain my heart* ....

Just before midnight I emptied water bucket over the porch railing, letting go of the past, clearing space for new beginnings. As if to salute that tradition, people across the lake gifted me with an incredible fireworks show. Reflections in the water were spectacular.

Wrapped like a late Christmas gift in a colorful quilt, I took extra chocolate outside for my inner child since I was skipping the sparklers—decided I was too mellow to play with matches. My inner child, my spirit self, and my mature woman united under stars brighter than any pyrotechnics. Neighborhood dogs were barking about the fireworks, the night air was laced with the faint scent of wood smoke, and the wisp of a crescent moon showed itself just above my rooftop. I felt the delicious chill of midnight and the magic of being wide awake, fully present in my body and very much alive on this special night.

May your next solo celebration be special, too.

***

Ursula's 51 and says she feels that age: ... *not in the sense of being old, but in the sense of being in full possession of myself.* This amazing woman is known and respected for her work on social justice issues; her career always has been about making a positive difference in our world. But the fact that men approach her at Home Depot, the supermarket and on the street has more to do with her good looks than her sharp mind or her work ethic. However, her intelligence and wit are likely to impress anyone she meets. Hers has been an earnest, conscious life journey, some of it challenging beyond belief. Ursula values her friends; most of them are women. Even when her eyes are sparkling with newfound love, she makes connection with close friends a priority. I'm proud to be one of them.

Ursula has been divorced now for almost three years after twenty-five years of marriage. I asked for her perspective on the challenges of marriage.

There are a lot of challenges. The biggest is that you inevitably get into grooves; some are good and helpful, others are unhealthy, boring, disappointing. ALL of them are very difficult to retread. And over 25 years people change a lot; it's hard to keep falling in love, especially when some changes are not good or healthy. Also, since a lot of things compete for your attention between 25 and 50, it's difficult not to put your relationship on hold for some periods of time. How long this goes without damage is tricky.

Responding to whether she'd like to marry again, *I'm not determined to, but would if it felt right. I'm open to it. I saw the benefits to my Dad and his wife of getting married in their 60's, so I have a good model. From my perspective right now—a relationship/partner is important to me—with or without marriage.*

She's dating now, has been in a relationship for several months. I asked how she's met men for dating.

A few friends have tried to fix me up; I've had a few men try to pick me up, literally on the street, but for the most part I have relied on internet dating services. Surprisingly, the friend match-ups have no advantages in terms of compatibility.

What are the positives and negatives of meeting new men this way?

Positives of internet dating: you have a lot of control—you determine how much access to let someone have; I've learned a lot about my feelings/expectations/wants in a partner and even more about myself and how different I am at 50 than I was 30 with regard to relationships—so much more open; the men I have met are all pretty much looking for the same thing—someone to be with, to trust, enjoy, care for—nothing weird or demanding or unrealistic. This was good news to someone who could have really shut down after an emotionally-wrenching divorce.

Using internet introductory services is the easiest way to meet lots of men. If I had relied on friends or chance encounters, I would not have had a quarter of the dates I've had in the last year. I found it fun to flirt by e-mail, instant messaging, phone—even when it fizzled. And the purpose is clear. People aren't on the sites unless they want to date; you don't have to guess like you do when you meet in person.

Disadvantages? *You need a thick skin or sense of humor. You won't meet most of the people you contact or are contacted by and—among those you meet—only a few turn into more than one date. Also, it seems a little weird to keep adjusting your perception of someone from profile to phone call to meeting. We naturally adjust perceptions as we get to know a person, but it's a little compressed in the internet scheme, so you can be very conscious of it. Actually you can get kind of possessed by it—compulsively checking emails, messages, matches, and so forth.*

What aspects of being married appeal to her most? *Lots of things. The bottom line for me on relationships and marriage is that both people should be better in them than they are alone—not just happier but better—being in partnership should help you explore different sides of your self in a safe place. A partner should give you peace, comfort, support, and confidence to do and be more than you would otherwise. If a relationship doesn't do that, I won't stay in it.*

It's nice being with someone after a good or bad day, cooking, sharing food, sleeping together ... fabulous, loving sex, laughing with someone, having someone reflect back to you your best and, gently, your worst features. And what's not to like? Having to accommodate someone else's schedule, feelings, quirks, lifestyle.

What about being single appeals to you most? *I like being solitary. I have lots of interests, and I like setting my own schedule for pursuing them. I'm comfortable doing things on my own, and I have lots of friends, so being lonely is not a concern.*

Least? *Being bored. Lack of intimacy in all senses of the word. And fearing no one would find the body until Monday when I didn't show up for work.*

Is she open to living with a "significant other" without marrying?

Yes. At my age I am smart enough to know that the unromantic stuff like money would have to be negotiated, with or without a civil or religious ceremony. So the formality of marriage would only come into play if I were very confident that the relationship was permanent —not just what's good for both of us now.

When I asked about her home, *I love my home. I think it's a real expression of my personality. I've recently undertaken some home improvements that make it even more my home. After the divorce, 'my home' took on the additional meaning of self sufficiency—tangible, fundamental evidence that I could manage on my own. I love that I own the home, that it's in my name. It was a particular point of satisfaction, a real marker of progress after the divorce—that I make the decisions about renovations and refinancing with confidence in my judgment. The feel of my home is calm and serene — very different from the decorating schemes in my other homes, even though I pretty much chose those colors/styles, too. Home is about being in my space—hence my surprise at how freely I have opened it to my special guy.*

On the subject of food, I have always cooked for myself, and I like to cook. Before I began seeing someone on a regular basis, I did get into a routine set of meals that were easy and enjoyable to me. I eat at the table or in front of the TV if something really good is on—so, rarely in front of TV. I never did the bachelor thing—pouring dressing on the salad wedge and eating over the sink, eating cold cereal for dinner, any kind of frozen dinners. One of the best parts of being in a steady relationship, though, has been the cooking. I really like having the 'excuse' and the audience to really cook. [Note: This woman is one of the finest cooks on the planet. I would walk over a bed of hot coals to get to her table.]

I ask about special things she does for herself, hoping to inspire living-single neophytes. *I always have fresh flowers in the house, which I buy, what's up with that? And I like wine and do not hesitate to open good stuff, a relative term that means more than $15 a bottle, when I am on my own. I'll cook special treats like lamb chops because even expensive food is pretty reasonable for one.*

About her career: *I work in community development—exciting, exhausting, frustrating but it's work I love. I feel bad for people who are counting the days, because I have always had work I felt was useful and important and that extended my skills. What else can you ask for? And I feel reasonably secure. I don't think there's anyone who doesn't fear the debilitating illness that can wipe you out financially as well as physically but I am glad, especially these days, to have some security, through both my job and savings.*

When I asked her to talk about pets: *I have had dogs—two of the greatest in the world, and it's hard to describe the connection one has to a great dog that you have raised. When I was feeling really alone after the divorce, my dog was a great companion to me. I don't have time for another dog now, and I feel the loss.*

About her comfort level when dining alone in restaurants, Ursula says. *I wouldn't say I feel comfortable going to very high-end restaurants alone.*

As big a foodie as I am, the idea of going to a nice restaurant includes someone to share the adventure with. But I don't mind going out to eat by myself, especially since I like sushi and not a lot of people in my life do. I sometimes take a magazine but find that I rarely read it when I go out. It didn't take practice for me because I was accustomed to eating out, going to movies on my own.

As far as going to events by myself, I'm kind of used to it. That was a learned skill because of work. I end up at a lot of dinners and galas and look for people I know to chat with, though not necessarily to hang out with; I would not call it fun. If I'm especially interested in an art event I will go by myself. The difference to me is that I don't extend the night if I go alone; I leave fairly early and go straight home. With a date or friend I would stop for a drink or something afterwards—take advantage of being out and dressed up. To tell the truth, the activities I forgo, with regret, are sporting events. Somehow going to a baseball game locally, let alone driving to Charlotte for a pro football game, is unappealing without a companion, and my girlfriends just don't get into the NFL like I do.

... I never feel diminished or unwelcome when I go to a party alone. And I have done the third wheel thing with one or two couples. They were good friends, so it wasn't too weird. The one strange thing that bugs me about being alone when I am at an event is having to get my own drink. Isn't that old fashioned? But I like having a man do the fetching when I am at a dress-up event, wedding or whatever.

I would like to say that having a spouse or date does not guarantee you will have a companion at the exhibit opening—and I would much rather go by myself to something like an opera or ballet than 'drag' a man who couldn't care less, or worse, is bored or half asleep!

I asked Ursula about marriage myths and myths about being single.

Hmmm myths about single women—you mean the cats, the long robes and fuzzy slippers? Actually, I'm not aware of myths about being a single woman—I have had some fears though. Here is an illustrative story. I went to the ballet by myself about four months after my divorce, looking forward to a big evening—at least a festive evening because of the particular performance and was disappointed at how empty the theater was. Then I noticed some women near me, maybe in their late 50s early 60s, and the three of them were wearing holiday shirts and sweaters with all kinds of tacky appliqués; I kind of sighed and hoped I wasn't looking into some future frumpy life. Then a woman three rows ahead of me turned around and I noticed her platinum hair framed a much older face than I anticipated and the outfit—wow! Way too much cleavage with accompanying wrinkles and sags bound in a top that was so age-inappropriate ... and I thought, jeez—I don't want to go down fighting that hard either. I hope to find a graceful way to mature into old age—but that did depress me.

Myths about marriage? *I don't know—maybe that it is normal for two people to spend 40-50 years together? That marriage 'makes people happy.'*

Parting thoughts on being single?

I had this insight the other day—two and a half years into my official singlehood. When I first realized I was going to be divorced after twenty-five years, it took a while, but eventually I accepted that I would have to start over again. At some point in the last year I realized I could now tell people that, at fiftyish, I got an opportunity to start over. That's really a cool thing—to recognize that I wasn't one of the many women who were just too tired, scared, lazy, or out of touch with their own feelings to say 'I am not going to settle for this; life is not nearly over. My life should be about more than grandkids, and I am going to start again with high expectations.'

***

The first time I met Bev, I thought she looked like a wonderstruck little girl. It was her petite stature, the pretty girl-next-door wholesomeness, and the impish smile that makes you wonder what merry mischief she's been up to. If I met her today, I'd think the same thing. She hasn't lost her ingénue looks over the years, even though life has worked her over pretty hard. Today she is relaxed, confident, and unassuming as ever. Unfailingly warm and caring, Bev takes life seriously; she doesn't take her ego-self seriously.

I was lucky to be visiting when she was honored for her service to the community through the practice of medicine. Bev understands that her patients' emotions, relationships, spirituality, and living conditions are significant in determining their well-being. She shares her warmth with them, respecting each individual and doing her best to honor their needs. She created a healing space away from the clinic, a nurturing environment for patients dealing with chronic and life-threatening illness. She often offers health-support programs for the community, and teaches chi gong classes herself.

Bev had survived a stunning betrayal in her marriage. As she worked through unimaginable turmoil, she stayed fully present with her turbulent emotions. And she managed not to wall off her heart after the breakup. She navigated the divorce trauma as she would a life threatening disease a few years later in an admirably conscious and courageous way.

After caring for so many patients for so many years, the doctor became the patient. She opted for traditional oncology treatments and explored the psychological, spiritual, and emotional aspects of what the disease meant for her. Bev used the same holistic approach for herself that she advocates for others. And she is healed; in fact, she's been back at full speed for several years now. These days it's a wiser "full speed" for this survivor.

Sidebar: I still smile thinking about Bev's "medical school marriage." She and her best friend-boyfriend had planned a trip to Disney World at the end of the term and they were sorely disappointed to realize they wouldn't have the funds they needed for the Disney adventure. But they had an idea: If they were to get married, they'd have money as wedding gifts from family, and then they could celebrate at Disney. Problem solved! They followed through on their plan, had a blast on the Disney honeymoon and divorced amicably three years later. They remain close friends to this day.

Bev's second marriage lasted seventeen years. She doesn't want to marry again, would not want to share her space.

I enjoy my life now more than I ever have and I've already used up more than half of it! She's not dating anyone but has *a primary relationship with a woman I travel with, shop with, and talk on the phone with every day. I have lots of other friends that I stay connected with, too, and enjoy some group activities with them.*

What about being single appeals to her most? *Having my own space to do my life.*

And least? *Well, sometimes you need somebody around to open a jar.*

About her home: *My home is paradise. It's in a beautiful location, and I've modified it to meet my needs. It's pet friendly, there's privacy for company, and it nourishes me. I can go out my door, and whatever direction I choose will be a distinctly different experience. The steep terrain makes each walk a conscious consideration; it's not rote. It keeps me healthy and offers a big dose of nature to balance internal stressors.*

I have a fabulous dog, Max, the love of my life. Sometimes my house is the neighborhood doggie day care, also known as Puppy Paradise. I have lots of fun watching them.

I asked about eating out, cooking at home, and whether she eats at the table or in front of TV. She's "pretty comfortable" about eating out alone now, but says it did take practice to get relaxed about it. She takes reading material when she dines out. And she does cook for herself, often sitting at the table and sometimes in front of TV. *I consider what I need to nourish myself; sometimes it's just the healthiest food I can find to squelch the hunger. At other times, I find satisfying hunger too time-and-energy-consuming, and I tend to ignore it.*

Something special she does for herself on a regular basis? *I take a long soak, with salts, in a full tub almost every night.*

About her marriage: *Being okay with letting go of a fantasy that wasn't showing up for me was harder than not being in a relationship. Letting go of the idea that it could be a lifelong, fantasy-driven situation was hard to do. Therefore, I stayed stuck in a bad situation longer than was good for me or my health.*

What would she say to women who are newly single or soon to be single?

Join or start a women's group; find friends who are comfortable being single; sign up for a class you're interested in and go to conferences or workshops that interest you. Some conferences and workshops are held at beautiful places and can be a learning vacation."

[Note: A retreat might be something to explore if you're looking for peace, healing, and growth. Have a look at Gleanings Foundation (in western North Carolina mountains) and the Sophia Institute (in Charleston, South Carolina).]

***

Rachel has been living independently for fifteen years, divorced after a twenty-four year marriage. She has a strong, healthy bond with her four adult children and grandchildren. And, even at sixty-four she's not someone you'd think of as "granny." I've known Rachel since early childhood. I admire her forthrightness and her ability to rise like the phoenix from the ashes of a bad marriage and some serious health challenges. She always makes a comeback, and she absolutely enjoys life—her own single life.

What aspects of marriage appealed to her? *The family being whole ... and sex.* The aspects she liked least? *Feeling trapped, not having money of my own, having no communication with my husband about important things.*

What does she see as myth, or myths, about marriage?

The myth I believed was right out of the Fifties—everything is wonderful and always ends with 'happily ever after.' Bullshit! We were all kidding ourselves, and so were our parents.

Her plan is to remain single, although she's open to having a man in her life for companionship. She has no doubt that she's happiest as a single woman.

I can do anything at any time without justification to anyone. Being in total control of self is important to me; men tend to cause me to give up self.

Having adult children with families of their own, the thought of marrying and bringing a whole other family into the picture and all the baggage and potential problems, I just don't need it at this point in my life. And it's just too damn much trouble to put up with men.

About her home, Rachel says, *Home is where I'm at my best. I built my home, and it's the best project I've ever completed. It's totally me. The things in my home are from family of origin, grandparents, and previous homes of mine. This gives me a feeling of continuity with the past. I'm very much attached to my home—its comfortable feeling, the surrounding scenery, and the neighborhood.*

Rachel enjoys her life without a career. Her divorce settlement left her financially secure, and she doesn't worry about resources for the future because she knows *it will all work out somehow.*

She doesn't usually dine out alone, but on the occasions she has, it's been okay.

I enjoy the social aspect though, being with friends and sharing a meal at a good restaurant. I also love to cook and enjoy eating what I prepare at home. It's a pleasure to cook for myself and others.

Going to parties and events alone is not a problem for me now, especially if I think I look good and know someone who will be there. I like being able to arrive and leave when I want and not having to worry about what a companion wants to do. When I was first single, going by myself was harder, so I mostly stayed home. Now I'm in control and make my decisions based on what I want to do rather than what others want me to do. There are lots of single women in my world now, so it's no big deal to go alone.

Rachel on the importance of her animal companions:

I don't remember a time when a dog wasn't part of my life. As a single woman, my dogs, one now deceased and one still going strong, have been my soul mates in a sense. I love them and they've loved me; in bad times they're always right there waiting for me to be okay again, understanding my pain and tears. I'll always have a dog. It would be too lonely without them in the house.

More from Rachel about being single:

Each of us is single for our own reasons, and each of us is different. A central theme of mine is that no matter what it takes, or how long it takes, until one is comfortable in her own skin, then being single will present problems. For me, the love of self begins with the love of God—Higher Power, Being.

I think single women need to want to take care of themselves or they will continue to seek someone to do it for them. The challenges of being single are no greater than those in a marriage. In all of life, there are peaks and valleys, good times, bad times, and so on. But if you have courage, maturity, and determination, you can overcome whatever comes your way with the help of faith, the support of family and a few accepting friends.

***

Phyllis is sixty-five, a happily retired teacher. She feels, and usually thinks of herself as, about forty-five. Married for fifteen years, she divorced and remained single for ten years.

She married again and became a widow after seven years. No children. She's been on her own for eleven years now.

Asked whether she would marry again, her response was clear:

Never. I see no advantages. I enjoy my independence, and I'm financially self-sufficient. Nothing about marriage appeals to me at this point. I don't like the idea of having somebody around all the time. I'm in a very comfortable relationship now with no strings, no pressure. My guy friend and I cook together and enjoy candlelight dinners three or four nights a week.

Phyllis loves her home, the house itself, the landscape, the location. She's happy there.

She enjoys having company. She likes keeping fresh flowers in the house and treats herself to special wines.

When I'm alone, I often eat in front of TV. I do cook for myself mostly; never stop at fast food places, and I don't go to restaurants by myself except for breakfast sometimes. I'm really not comfortable going alone to parties or other events. It has a lot to do with driving, parking, and so forth at night.

"You always will be taken care of once you're married" is the myth Phyllis was sold. That will sound familiar to many women of her vintage.

Any words of wisdom for other women?

Don't always be looking for someone. It's better to just 'let it happen.' Don't ever think you can change someone. Know that no one is perfect, and there will always be things you don't like about a person. Those things might not show up in the beginning, but they will come out eventually. When you begin to grow as an individual, you will change in some ways your friends and family will notice. And that's just normal.

***

Lucy, at sixty-five, feels ageless most of the time. She was married for thirteen years and now single for more than twenty. She's into energy management now—her own. She enjoys making things beautiful: her home, a vase of flowers or a blank canvas.

Here's what she liked and didn't like about being married.

First of all, it's been so long since I was married, I barely remember what it felt like to be half of a couple. The good stuff? *The early euphoria of being in love, mostly with love, in the beginning, and 'playing house' were nice. Sex was a novelty, and only with one's husband was it acceptable in my world. But best was the joy of bringing life into the world and being a family—that was good. I try not to waste time on regrets and rarely do. But it would have been great if it had worked out to keep an intact family.*

I didn't recognize negative aspects until the marriage began to deteriorate. I pretty much tried to be whatever he needed at a given time. I never thought about independence. I left my parents' home to get married, never lived independently until after my divorce.

Now I have a long list of things I wouldn't want to give up to be married.

Like what? *Being responsible only for and to myself; not having to justify how I spend money; making my own plans to suit me, often on the spur of the moment.*

And what if you're unhappy, going through a rough patch? Do you miss having on-site support?

I'm generally happy. And I can't say that I got much emotional support in my marriage. In all fairness, back then I expected my husband to read my mind or to know me completely because he was my husband. How naive was that? He wasn't an uncaring person, just not psychic. Not especially sensitive either.

As the marriage was ending, I was terribly lonely all the time. I thought about something Marilyn Monroe supposedly said: 'If I'm going to be alone, I'd rather be by myself.' That's pretty much my motto today.

Lucy's take on marital myths?

The whole Cinderella thing; a man would rescue me, take care of me, and give me a beautiful life. A family. Happiness. Protection. There was the myth that men are much stronger than women and generally 'better.' Ha! I'm sure younger women would find it hard to imagine that we believed all that. I wouldn't want to know what they think of us. They are more plugged in to reality than we were. Men are physically stronger in most cases, but that's about where the superiority ends. I think women are usually stronger emotionally and in other ways. But generally we're on fairly equal footing.

What do I like about being single? Nearly everything. But it took me a long time to get comfortable with the idea. No prince was coming to awaken this sleeping princess. It was up to me to make my own life and my own happiness. After all, who knows better how to create a good life for us? Fear was an impediment to my growth for a long time, but even early in my single years, I grew in spite of myself. Just through the demands of day to day circumstances.

For a long time after the divorce I didn't allow myself to get involved with a man— except a good friend from work who was also divorced. We went out occasionally. But I wouldn't entertain the idea of a serious relationship. I wasn't willing to further complicate my children's lives. The breakup of our family was more than enough to deal with. Yes, I've had a couple of relationships since I've lived alone. It would be fun to have a man-friend to go out for dinner with, or dancing. Incidentally, I know married women who wish for that, too! No, I don't want anybody moving into my home, and I don't plan on leaving it.

I have some fabulous friends. They are my so-called 'soft place to fall' and, hopefully, I am the same for them.

Advice for other women? *I don't feel qualified to advise, but that never stopped me. Let's see: Keep your friends close. Learn to give and receive. Get to know yourself. Be good to yourself, as good as you are to the person you love most in the world. And laugh. Do whatever it takes to give yourself laughter. It feels good, it's not illegal, and doesn't hurt anyone. Say yes when you mean yes and no when you mean no. If you don't know about boundaries and setting them to take care of yourself, learn. Start learning now.*

Find whatever you do that absorbs you so intensely that you lose track of time. That's what I call 'a passion.' Give it room to grow. Find something outside yourself that you can do to make the world a little better. But only something that gives back to you; it's not the right thing if it zaps your energy.

Most of all, listen to that inner voice—your intuition. Whatever you call it, it's there. The more you listen, the more you will recognize its guidance, and the more you will learn to trust it.

***

Kathryn, in her sixties, is single and enjoys her career. I asked her to tell me about her work.

I'm licensed as a nurse and professional counselor. For thirty years my primary job was in cardiovascular care. The main focus was teaching the nursing staff how to care for heart patients and teaching heart patients and their families how to take care of themselves at home. I went back to school in my mid-forties and did post-masters work in counseling. For about fourteen years, I had a second job in the pastoral counseling department at my hospital. I worked one or two evenings a week doing counseling. About five years ago, I became a part of the research staff.

Enjoy your job or counting the days until retirement?

I like my job, but I would like to retire. I won't be able to do that for a while though, because the expenses of modernizing my house can't be handled on a fixed income. But next year I'll be receiving Social Security and able to cut back to two or three days at work. I can hardly wait to have more time to spend at home.

What aspects of being single appeal to you most? *My independence and quiet time. Least? Not having someone else around to help with chores that are difficult for me or that require handyman expertise—not that every man has handyman skills.*

Kathryn did most of her dating in her twenties and thirties. By the time she got into her forties she had "stopped checking out the ring finger" of men she met. She was satisfied with the quality of her single life and not seeking to change it. Comfortable going alone into any social situation, she's never felt awkward on her own, even at finer restaurants. *I know I haven't always been as sure of myself as I am now. But, according to my mother, I've always had a mind of my own and a large independent streak. Most of my friends are married, but I never feel like a fifth wheel when I'm the only one who's not a couple. Since I'm fine with my singleness, they don't feel awkward either.*

Kathryn said something that gave me a valuable insight: *I took the Myers-Briggs test in 1983 when I was in the middle of burnout at work.*

Learning I was an introvert living in an extrovert world (and trying to keep up) revolutionized my life and helped me recuperate from the burnout.

It was so freeing to start living as an introvert and empowering not to apologize for being different. The Myers-Briggs definition of an introvert is not at all related to the wallflower image we tend to have. The Myers-Briggs definition is explained by the answer to this question: 'How do you get re-energized when you have that need?' For me, it was definitely NOT being with other people in a social situation.

I have said for decades that I'm very often alone but don't remember ever being lonely. There's a significant difference, and I see my desire for solitude and singleness as a gift. I'm super-glad I don't have anyone living with me in my little cocoon. When I want companionship, I have a best friend and several other close friends who are never too busy to talk or spend time with me. And that is a wonderful gift.

I asked Kathryn about her home: *I love my home, 'warts and all!' I'm in the 85-year-old home I grew up in, still sleep in my old bedroom. Needless to say, there are constant renovations and repairs, and I'm not sure I will ever have the money to get it updated to the extent I'd like. All the work I've done doesn't take away the character and charm of my childhood home though. I'm just making it safe and user-friendly for the rest of my life, even if I should have disabilities. My memories of home, childhood, and family are precious to me.*

Do you prepare meals and enjoy them at the table, or are you inclined to eat take-out in front of TV?

I like to cook. And I have an eclectic collection of dishes—good china and everyday china—that I enjoy using, never disposables. I browse in department and thrift stores, looking for dishes and linens on sale. Most of them don't match at all, but I love the patterns. Many have the blue and yellow color scheme of my kitchen-dining room, and two patterns have place settings for twenty. One set is for Christmas, so I use those when all the family gathers at my house, as we will this year. I eat every meal at my big dining room table. Not a fan of TV, she rarely watches.

Kathryn's love of home resonates in her responses. She enjoys flowers, cut flowers in a vase and the container gardens she tends on both porches. The wild birds she feeds are her only pets now, unless you count the chameleon spending the winter in an empty pot on her front porch.

Meaningful relationships and my solitude are the most important things to me. And, for me, having a very personal relationship with God is the key to a meaningful life. There are too many things bigger than I am—things that can only be handled by somebody bigger than any human, no matter how bright or talented.

Kathryn loves her life, simple and single by design. I almost can hear her saying *I'm super-glad I don't have anyone living with me in my little cocoon.*

***

On Living Independently

Ever look for shells when you're wading in the ocean as incoming waves stir up the bottom sand, clouding the water? When that's happening, there is no way to see shells in the churning surf. But if you stay focused there will be, between the waves, a moment of clarity. The water becomes still and perfectly clear, making everything visible. That's when you're most likely to be rewarded for your patience.

The turbulence and that moment of clarity could be a metaphor for my own thinking. For me, the turbulence comes in cycles, and there's nearly always a lesson to be learned from whatever it is I'm dealing with. After *I don't know how many* of these periods of struggle, I learned to acknowledge the experience by asking, "What is it I'm feeling? Where are the feelings coming from? What can I learn from this?" If I ask those questions, the answers come. Maybe not instantly or in the way I'd expect, but I become clear enough to get unstuck and begin moving forward.

I've gone through periods of confusion about having a man in my life— ranging from ambivalence to longing to deep sadness, to peace— simultaneously or alternating in a mix much like the churning sand. Thinking gets cloudy. Emotions are turbulent. When I accept whatever feelings I'm experiencing, rather than fighting, judging, or denying them, clarity will come. It always does. Sometimes I just have to be more patient than I want to be.

Sidebar: "It's a blast!" Ursula is talking about her on-line dating adventures. I'm not sure whether I'm more stunned by her enthusiasm or the fact that the word "blast" has found its way into the vocabulary of my serious, articulate friend.

She thinks I should try it. I remind her I did try it, back when she was busy being married. It was a nightmare. She says I should try again, just have fun this time. What does she think my intention was last time? I had decided that the last time *was* the last time for me.

But Ursula's powers of persuasion won. I decided to beat my toes with the internet dating hammer one more time.

When you sign up for an online service, you answer a lot of questions. Multiple choice questions that make me crazy, Why? Because "Yes, this is partially true sometimes but not always the case" is not allowed.

Then there's the narrative you write about yourself, the profile. I wanted to present myself accurately. In fact, I might be the only person in the history of these introduction services who told the truth about my age. Somebody said that was a mistake. *Why was that a mistake? How can you believe that a person who lies about age will tell the truth about other things?*

I signed up for three months. When the first batch of "matches" arrived at my in-box, the most attractive fellow by far was a favorite older cousin. I swear. Somehow he had become years younger and acquired skills and attributes that were news to me. Also in the first batch was a man who had pursued me for a couple of years and who now knows I actually *am* available. In the first and subsequent batches were also men who looked my father's age and claimed to be my age or younger. Some looked like a better match for *America's Most Wanted* than for me.

Actually I did get some e-mails. A few were from men looking for a path to citizenship or a sugah mama. One gorgeous guy in his late twenties said, *You r butiful ladee. i lik you to met my son he is 5. his mother she die. please writ me bak.* I felt a rush of compassion just before hitting the "delete" key.

And to be honest, I did meet a couple of men— once.

But what was I thinking, signing up for the online dating thing again? I remember when I bought those uncomfortable shoes to wear to dinner with a man I was meeting for the first time and trying not to limp. All because my friend said, "They show off your great legs" ...What?! Why had I gotten advice on what to wear? Jeeez, I'm not fifteen. Or fifty, for that matter. How could I package myself like some object on eBay? Had I fallen into the old validation-by-man trap that snared me in my twenties and thirties?

I told a friend that over 400 men had looked at my profile and photos on the dating site and essentially said "no thanks." They don't charge extra for that humiliating information. My friend blew it off, but I pressed, "Come on, if that same thing happened to you, what would you think?" She said, "I'd think they were all jerks!" And she meant that. Even though I've run into my share of jerks, the idea of 400 of them checking out my profile seemed like a real stretch.

As I began sorting out my feelings about the experience, I had to laugh. I was thinking of my recent man-search in terms of a dog chasing cars. If the dog ever caught the car, whatever would she do with it? LOL.

My friend Carol says her on-line experience was like a post-graduate course in men, whereas I learned more about myself than about men. As I've said, my mantra has been "It would take a very special man to take the place of no man at all," and that remains true today. Unlike Leila, "walking on water" wouldn't be on my list of criteria, but let's just say he'd have to be the best swimmer imaginable.

While my internet dating exercise was excruciating, several friends have found fun, love, and even husbands to show for their courage in "getting out there." So, take heart that I'm more the exception than the rule if you're thinking of signing up. Those friends are sorry I can't "just have fun" with it, see it as "an adventure." Sorry, I'm all done. If I'm ever tempted to wade into the online waters again, someone please push me into the alligator pond out back. Now *that* would be an adventure.

When I stay as honest with myself as I am with others, it's clear that my life "as is" would be pretty hard to beat. And I'm clear that a relationship, for me, wouldn't include living together full-time. Visits at his place and mine might work. I'm with my friend Lexy who said, "Live close by, visit often" makes sense to her.

I'm a fortunate woman with a home I love. Mother Nature's gifts feed my spirit daily at my version of Walden Pond. I don't want anyone disturbing my peace. I'm free to choose silence and birdsong over TV or music, or I can choose electronic sounds, loud as I want or as soft. I have phenomenal friends, a fabulous son, granddaughter, and daughter-in-law, each as close to perfect as we humans get. My mother is 87, and I enjoy having time with her. I usually can find companionship if I'm craving company, by phone if not in person.

I need solitude more than most people I know. So, my "living single" perspective is different than that of women who are less reclusive. You heard from some of those women earlier.

I've lived alone for nearly thirty years, so it's gotten pretty comfortable. And I'm mindful about the danger of turning a comfortable life into a rut. I remind myself there's little difference between a rut and a grave: A grave is just a little deeper.

Grateful to have financial resources that meet *my not too materialistic needs*, I'm trusting the resources will last as long as I do. I've learned to take pretty good care of myself and, thankfully, I'm healthy. I know how to celebrate special occasions, even when I'm alone. And I know how to *make* occasions special. I have no problem going just about anywhere on my own now: parties, plays, dinner, some road trips, activities with friends. I often dance alone at home, but, yes, it is better to have a partner in public. [Have a listen to Keb Mo's "She Just Wants to Dance" and see if you can sit still.]

Remember, I had the benefit of a good therapist to help me understand and accept who I am, to identify and deal with my feelings. With arduous work in therapy, an ongoing support group, and the gift of grace, I've grown in love, compassion, and respect for myself. I'm usually comfortable, as they say, in my own skin—warts, cellulite and all. I'll continue to welcome into my world anyone who can expand my life experience in a positive way and who will allow me to expand his. What I'm not looking for is someone to "complete" me.

My energy level and attitudes are younger than my years indicate, but this last birthday brought some turbulence around the idea of a relationship with a significant other. Only recently did it begin to settle and clear.

And this time it was about *not having a significant other*—wait, that's not true—my life is rich in significant others. Restated: I'm getting clearer and more accepting about not having the love of a special man in Act 3 of my life. I realized I had somehow thought there would be.

The clarifying question I asked myself was, "Am I telling myself the truth about wanting a man to share my life, my space, time, energy, family, friends and thoughts, every day?"

Here's what I know now: Even if I had a fabulous man in my daily life, the passion would likely fade. But when you're madly, deeply in love with Life itself, the passion renews itself and surprises you at every turn. It doesn't get dull or routine.

My young granddaughter not only expresses the kind of love I'm talking about here, she embodies it. E.G. is love without self-consciousness. Love illuminates her, causes her merry blue eyes to sparkle. She kisses the cold, metal egret sculptures in my house and touches rocks and shells with great reverence when she visits. To feel and express love like that surely must be Nirvana.

Young children like E.G. "get it." They live immersed in the present moment. They express aliveness from the heart, not the judging mind which is a wrecking ball to ecstasy. When I'm fully awake, aware in the present moment, when I let go of self-consciousness about my exuberance, when I'm true to my Self above all else, I am *exactly* like E.G. The world is fresh and delicious in each unfolding moment. I'm ecstatically in love with Life. I believe I will have few regrets when it's time for me to leave this world; that's because I will know, for sure, that I have danced my own dance on *this* planet.

There's an abundance of love in this amazing world, more than enough for all of us. Maybe it didn't come in the package we ordered, but it's here in this very moment. We only need to wake up, embrace the love, and dance to the music of Life.

Dream Yourself

Dream yourself a big dream,
Then wake up and follow it
Down the soft lichen lane
And over the cockle shells
Where dolphins call.

Go where the blue flamingo drinks
Gin, where saints are partial to jazz.
Jump over the stumbling blocks
Or fly over, wishing a good day
To the snails taking their time
On the way to Wherever.

Push the boulder aside
With one finger
And blink yourself

Into the cave.
Trust the light to appear
Once you commit. Begin
To feel your way along
The centuries-pocked wall.

Sure enough, bats wearing
miner's hats light your way
To the gemstones. You take
The big one, a diamond
Encrusted in purple clay.

Now you hitch a ride
With a dragonfly to the next
Part of the dream, waving
And blowing kisses
Like a beauty queen to
The crowd at a parade.

You throw your head back
Laughing when the spotted horse
Invites you to climb on
And go the distance.
Dream yourself a big dream,
Then wake up and follow it.

About the Title:

Over time, dreams have given me guidance, warnings, answers, inspiration, and comfort, and I always pay attention. Sometimes I have to work at understanding dream symbols. At other times a message will be unmistakably clear. Important messages often seem to come in nightmares, since frightening images are more easily remembered.

I like it when people tell me their dreams, and I was happy when my mother shared this: She dreamed she was visiting Mars and suddenly was told it was time to go. She protested that she wasn't ready to leave because she had wanted to dance there. She could stay no longer. Her ship was sailing, so to speak. In the dream she was disappointed not to experience dancing on Mars.

For my mother, this was only a strange dream. For me it was a reminder to celebrate life and honor what my heart tells me is important. *Now.* It was a call to be fully present to life as it is happening in each moment, to enjoy "dancing" while I'm here. That way, there will be no regrets when it's time to leave *this* planet.

May you learn from your dreams and enjoy your own unique dance.

Author's Note:

Throughout the book, names have been changed. I promised anonymity to the women and couples in the *Married* and *Single* sections; thus, they felt free to share their insights generously and honestly. Names and identifying information also were changed to honor the privacy of others. This was done so that I could be candid in talking about the meaningful roles others have played in my life.

Discussion Questions

For Group Discussion or Personal Reflection

On Living Married/Partnered or Living Solo

What aspects of being married/partnered or single appeal to you most?

What aspects of your married/partnered/single life do you find challenging?

Whatever your relationship status, are you comfortable having dinner alone at a nice restaurant? Attending parties, concerts on your own? Vacationing?

When you're home alone, do you prepare meals and enjoy eating alone, or are you more likely to have takeout or cereal in front of TV?

Do you allow yourself special treats (flowers, good wines or coffees); do you nurture yourself with rest, music, quiet time, hobbies? Does your relationship status influence the things you allow yourself to do/have? How might you enrich your life by claiming more "me" time?

What does "home" mean to you? Do you feel relaxed and nurtured there? What could you do to make your home a clearer reflection of who you are?

If you're currently married/partnered and found yourself suddenly alone, would you want to remarry or live with a significant other? Why or why not?

On Growing Toward Greater Authenticity

Someone makes a mean-spirited comment that you find offensive.

How do you respond?

You've been looking forward to a beach retreat with close friends; you learn that a sibling is hosting a family reunion that same weekend. Your preference for the retreat is strong, and so is the family pressure. What do you do?

How much do the opinions of others affect the way you present yourself to the world? Are you more interested in being liked or being respected by others?

Do you tell the truth even when it's uncomfortable? Are there ever reasons not to speak truthfully? If you know you've been wrong, do you say so or let it slide?

What's one thing you could do change in order to live your life more authentically?

Think of a time you said "yes" when you wanted to say "no," or a time you said "no" when you wanted to say "yes." Do you know why you responded as you did? Would your answer be different today? If so, why?

About the Author

Lucinda Shirley lives on a Lowcountry lake in her native South Carolina, surrounded by ancient oaks and amazing wildlife.

A member of the South Carolina Writers Workshop and the Southeastern Writers Association, Lucinda is a freelance writer, poet, and writing coach. Her work can be found in magazines, literary journals, and online blogs. When she was named first and second place winner in a SCWW poetry competition, she was relieved to learn there had been other entries. *Dancing on Mars* is her first book.

You can reach Lucinda at dancingonmars@yahoo.com or visit her at: lucindashirleydancingonmars.blogspot.com/ and poetrypeddler.blogspot.com.

ALL THINGS THAT MATTER PRESS ™

FOR MORE INFORMATION ON TITLES AVAILABLE FROM
ALL THINGS THAT MATTER PRESS, GO TO
http://allthingsthatmatterpress.com
or contact us at
allthingsthatmatterpress@gmail.com

14197939R00123

Made in the USA
Lexington, KY
27 May 2012